A Narrative of the Mutiny, on Board the Ship Globe, of Nantucket, in the Pacific Ocean, Jan. 1824
by William Lay

A
NARRATIVE
OF THE
MUTINY,
ON BOARD THE
SHIP GLOBE,
OF NANTUCKET,
IN THE
PACIFIC OCEAN, JAN. 1824.
AND THE
JOURNAL
OF A
RESIDENCE OF TWO YEARS
ON THE
MULGRAVE ISLANDS;
WITH OBSERVATIONS ON THE MANNERS AND
CUSTOMS OF THE INHABITANTS.

BY WILLIAM LAY, OF SAYBROOK, CONN. AND
CYRUS M. HUSSEY, OF NANTUCKET:
The only Survivors from the Massacre of the Ship's Company by the Natives.

NEW-LONDON:
PUBLISHED BY WM. LAY, AND C. M. HUSSEY.

1828.

TO JOHN PERCIVAL, Esq.

OF THE U. S. NAVY;

Who, under the auspices of Government, visited the Mulgrave Islands, to release the survivors of the Ship Globe's crew, and extended to them every attention their unhappy situation required—the following Narrative is most respectfully dedicated, by

WILLIAM LAY, &
CYRUS M. HUSSEY,
The Authers.

S. Green, Printer.

This book is a reprint of the volume described on the title page, and is issued by The Abbey Press, Publishers, 114 Fifth Avenue, New York, London, Montreal, and elsewhere

THE YOUNG MUTINEER.

His sun rose unclouded and brightly it shone
In the pride of the morning and promised a noon
Of glory and gladness; it sank to the flood
In blackness and blindness, and tarnished by
     blood.
Disowned and dishonored its last gloomy glare
Was shed on the grave of the young mutineer.

Tho' beardless his cheek, yet his was a soul
That knew not a master, that brooked no control;
Tho' beardless his cheeks, yet his was a hand
Acquainted with daggers; a voice to command,
An eye that wept, a heart without fear,
Were the pride and the boast of the young
     mutineer.

He lies on the beach of a lone desert isle,
His dirge the green billows are chanting the
     while,

▼

The Young Mutineer.

'As they in wild tumult, roll over his head,
And wash the high rock, that marks out his wet
      bed;
There lies with a heart that ne'er knew a fear,
The mangled remains of the young mutineer.

He lies on the beach, the cold waters beside,
And dreadful and dark was the death that he died
No mother mourns o'er him, no fond fair one
      weeps
Where far from the land of his father he sleeps.
But the rude swelling wave, and the sea birds
      career
On the wet sandy grave of the young mutineer.

He lies on the beach by a comrade in guilt,
His forehead was cloven, his best blood spilt.
The cries of his victims have risen to God,
'And their wailings were quenched
In the murderer's blood.
He fell without mourners, for none dropped a
      tear
O'er the mangled remains of the young mutineer.

The Young Mutineer.

He lies on the beach, where the weeds and the
    shells,
Mark the bounds of the sea, where in tumult it
    swells
They scooped him a grave, and there laid him
    at rest,
And heaped the wet sand on his bare, bloody
    breast.
And they rolled a huge rock and planted it there
To mark the lone grave of the young mutineer.

In years that are coming the seamen will tell
Of murders and murdered, and murderer's yells.
The tale, the lone watch of night will beguile
When they sail by the shores of that desolate isle.
And their beacon shall be, as they thitherward
    steer,
The black rock on the grave of the young
    mutineer.

HENRY GLOVER.

INTRODUCTION.

FORMERLY whales were principally taken in the North Seas: the largest were generally found about Spitzbergen or Greenland, some of them measuring ninety feet in length. At the commencement of the hazardous enterprise of killing whales, before they had been disturbed by man,, they were so numerous in the bays and harbors, that when taken the blubber was for the most part boiled into oil upon the contiguous coast.

The pure oil and whalebone were only preserved in those days; consequently a ship could carry home the product of a greater number of whales than a ship of the same size now can. Indeed, so plentiful were the whales in those seas, and taken with such facility, that the ships employed were not sufficient to carry home the oil and bone, and other ships were often sent to

bring home the surplus quantity. But the coasts
of these countries were soon visited by ships
from Denmark, Hamburg and Holland, as well
as from England; and from frequently being
killed in the shoal water near the coasts, the
whales gradually receded from the shores, and
have since been found only in deeper water, and
at a much greater distance from the land.

In the earlier stages of the whale fishery,
of which we are now treating, the ships were
generally on the whaling waters early in May,
and whether successful or not they were obliged
to commence their return by the succeeding
August, to avoid the early accumulation of ice
in those seas. But it not unfrequently happened, that ships procured and returned with a
cargo in the months of June and July, making a
voyage only about three months, whereas a voyage to the Pacific Ocean is now often protracted
to three years!

Among the early whalers it was customary to
have six boats to a ship, and six men to a boat, besides the harpooner. What at that time was

Introduction.

considered an improved method in killing whales, consisted in discharging the harpoon from a kind of swivel; but it was soon found to be attended with too much inconvenience to be much practised, and the muscular arms and steady nerves of the harpooner have ever since performed the daring duty, of first striking the whale. The ropes attached to the harpoon used to be about 200 fathoms in length, and some instances occurred, that all the lines belonging to six boats were fastened together, and ran out by one whale, the animal descending in nearly a perpendicular line from the surface. Instead of going prepared to bring home a shipload of oil, it was customary to bring only the blubber, and instead of trying the oil out and putting it into casks on board, the fat of the whale was cut up into suitable pieces, pressed hard in tubs carried out for the purpose, and in this position was the return cargo received at home.

Of so great consequence was the whale fishery considered to Great Britain, that a bounty of 40s. for every ton, when the ship was 200 tons, or

Introduction.

upwards, was given to the crews of ships engaged in that business in the Greenland seas, under certain conditions. But this bounty was found to draw too largely upon the treasury; and while the subject was under consideration in the British Parliament, in 1786, it was stated that the sums which that country had paid in bounties to the Greenland fishers, amounted to 1,265,461 pounds sterling. Six thousand seamen were employed in that fishery, and each cost the government £13 10s. per annum. The great encouragement given to that branch of commerce, caused so large a number to engage in it, that the oil market became glutted, and it was found necessary to export considerable quantities.

In 1786, the number of British ships engaged in the whale fishery to Davis's Strait and the Greenland seas was 139, besides 15 from Scotland. In 1787, notwithstanding the bounty had been diminished, the number of English ships was 217, and the following year 222.

The charter right of the island of Nantucket was bought by Thomas Mayhew, of Watertown,

Introduction.

of Joseph Ferrick, steward to Lord Sterling, in
1641 ; and afterwards sold to Tristam Coffin, and
his associates, who settled upon it in 1659.   On
the 10th of May, 1660, Sachems, Wonnock, and
Nickannoose, for and in behalf of the nations of
the Island in consideration of the sum of £25,
conveyed by deed about half of the Island
to the first ten purchasers, who afterwards took
in other associates.

Whaling from Nantucket was first carried on
from the shore in boats.   In 1672, James Loper
entered into a contract with the inhabitants of
the Island, for the purpose of prosecuting the
whale fishery, by which it appears that James
Loper agreed to be one third in the enterprise,
and sundry other people of the Island, the other
two thirds, in everything connected with the undertaking.   It. was further stipulated, that for
every whale killed by any one of the contracting
party, the town should receive five shillings, and
for the encouragement of James Loper, the town
granted him ten acres of land in some convenient
situation, and liberty for the commonage of

Introduction.

three cows, twenty sheep, and one horse, with necessary wood and water for his use, on condition that he should follow the trade of whaling for two years, build upon his land, etc., etc.

Thus it will be seen that the commencement of whaling at Nantucket, was on a very small scale, and practised only along the shores of the Island; whereas, at this time, our ships leave no seas unexplored in pursuit of these monsters of the deep. We might pursue the subject through the various stages of improvement up to this time, but it would swell this introduction beyond the limits designed. It is proper, however, to observe that the present number of ships employed in the whale fishery from Nantucket, is about 70, averaging about 350 tons each, and manned by about 1,500 seamen.

THE GLOBE MUTINY.

CHAPTER I.

THE ship Globe, on board of which vessel occurred the horrid transactions we are about to relate, belonged to the Island of Nantucket; she was owned by Messrs. C. Mitchell & Co., and other merchants of that place; and commanded on this voyage by Thomas Worth, of Edgartown, Martha's Vineyard. William Beetle (mate), John Lumbard (2d mate), Nathaniel Fisher, (3d mate), Gilbert Smith (boat steerer), Samuel B. Comstock (boat steerer), Stephen Kidder (seaman), Peter C. Kidder (seaman), Columbus Worth (seaman), Rowland Jones (seaman), John Cleveland, (seaman), Constant Lewis (seaman), Holden Henman (seaman), Jeremiah Ingham (seaman), Joseph Ignasius Prass (sea-

15

The Globe Mutiny.

man), Cyrus M. Hussey (cooper), Rowland Coffin (cooper), George Comstock (seaman), and William Lay (seaman).

On the 15th day of December, we sailed from Edgartown, on a whaling voyage to the Pacific Ocean, but in working out, having carried away the cross-jack-yard, we returned to port and after having refitted and sent aloft another, we sailed again on the 19th, and on the same day anchored in Holmes' Hole. On the following day a favorable opportunity offering to proceed to sea, we got under way, and after having cleared the land, discharged the pilot, made sail, and performed the necessary duties of stowing the anchors, unbending and coiling away the cables, etc. On the 1st of January, 1823, we experienced a heavy gale from N. W., which was but the first in the catalogue of difficulties we were fated to encounter. As this was our first trial of a seaman's life, the scene presented to our view, "'Mid the howling storm," was one of terrific grandeur, as well as of real danger. But as the ship scudded well, and the wind was fair, she was kept before it, under a close reefed main-top-sail and fore-sail, although during the gale, which lasted forty-eight hours, the sea frequently threatened to board us, which was prevented by the skillful management of the helm. On the 9th of January, we made the Cape Verde Islands, bearing S. W., twenty-five miles distant, and on the 17th, crossed the Equator. On the 29th of the same month we saw sperm whales, lowered our boats, and succeeded in taking one; the blubber of which, when boiled out, yielded us seventy-five barrels of oil. Pursuing our voyage, on the 23d of February we passed the Falkland Islands, and about the 5th of March, doubled the great promontory of South America, Cape Horn, and stood to the Northward.

We saw whales once only before we reached the Sandwich Islands, which we made on the 1st of May, early in the morning. When drawing in with the island of Hawaii about four in the afternoon, the man at the masthead gave notice that he saw a shoal of black fish on the lee bow; which we soon found to be canoes on their way to meet us. It falling calm at this time prevented their getting alongside until night-fall, which they did, at a distance of more than three leagues from the land. We received from them a very welcome supply of potatoes, sugar-cane, yams, cocoanuts, bananas, fish, etc., for which we gave them in return, pieces of iron hoop, nails, and similar articles. We stood off and on during the next day, and after obtaining a sufficient supply of vegetables and fruit, we shaped our course for Oahu, at which place we arrived on the following day, and after lying there twenty hours, sailed for the coast of Japan, in company with the whaling ships Palladium of Boston and Pocahontas of Falmouth; from which ships we parted company when two days out. After cruising in the Japan seas several months, and obtaining five hundred and fifty barrels of oil, we again shaped our course for the Sandwich Islands, to obtain a supply of vegetables, etc.

While lying at Oahu, six of the men deserted

in the night; two of them having been retaken were put in irons, but one of them having found means to divest himself of his irons, set the other at liberty, and both escaped.

To supply their places, we shipped the following persons, viz.: Silas Payne, John Oliver, Anthony Hanson, a native of Oahu, Wm. Humphries, a black man, and steward, and Thomas Liliston. Having accommodated ourselves with as many vegetables and as much fruit as could be preserved, we again put to sea, fondly anticipating a successful cruise, and a speedy and happy meeting with our friends.

After leaving Oahu we ran to the south of the Equator, and after cruising a short time for whales without much success, we steered for Fannings Island, which lies in lat. 3° 49′ N., and long. 158° 29′ W. While cruising off this island an event occurred which, whether we consider the want of motives, or the cold-blooded and obstinate cruelty with which it was perpetrated, has not often been equalled. We speak of the want of motives, because although

The Globe Mutiny.

some occurrences which we shall mention, had given the crew some ground for dissatisfaction, there had been no abuse or severity which could in the least degree excuse or palliate so barbarous a mode of redress and revenge. During our cruise to Japan the season before, many complaints were uttered by the crew among themselves, with respect to the manner and quantity in which they received their meat, the quantity sometimes being more than sufficient for the number of men, and at others not enough to supply the ship's company; and it is fair to presume that the most dissatisfied deserted the ship at Oahu.

But the reader will no doubt consider it superfluous for us to attempt an unrequired vindication of the conduct of the officers of the Globe, whose aim was to maintain a correct discipline which should result in the furtherance of the voyage and be a benefit to all concerned, more especially when he is informed, that part of the men shipped at Oahu, in the room of the deserters, were abandoned wretches,

The Globe Mutiny.

who frequently were the cause of severe reprimands from the officers, and in one instance one of them received a severe flogging. The reader will also please to bear in mind, that Samuel B. Comstock, the ringleader of the mutiny, was an officer (being a boat-steerer), and as is customary, ate in the cabin. The conduct and deportment of the captain toward this individual, was always decorous and gentlemanly, a proof of intentions long premeditated to destroy the ship. Some of the crew were determined to leave the ship provided she touched at Fannings Island, and we believe had concerted a plan of escape, but of which the perpetration of a deed chilling to humanity, precluded the necessity. We were at this time in company with the ship Lyra, of New Bedford, the captain of which had been on board the Globe during the most of the day, but had returned in the evening to his own ship. An agreement had been made by him with the captain of the Globe, to set a light at midnight as a signal for tacking. It may not be amiss to acquaint the reader of the manner in which whalemen keep watch during the night. They generally carry three boats, though some carry four, five, and sometimes six; the Globe, however, being of the class carrying three. The captain, mate, and second mate stand no watch, except there is blubber to be boiled; the boat-steerers taking charge of the watch and managing the ship with their respective boat's crews, and in this instance dividing the night into three parts, each taking a third. So it happened that Smith, after keeping the first watch, was relieved by Comstock (whom we shall call by his surname in contradistinction to his brother George), and the waist boat's crew, and the former watch retired below to their berths and hammocks. George Comstock took the helm, and during his trick, received orders from his brother to "keep the ship a good full," swearing that the ship was too nigh the wind. When his time at the helm had expired he took the rattle (an instrument used by whalemen to announce the expiration of the hour, the watch, etc.), and began to shake it, when Comstock came to him, and in the most peremptory manner, ordered him to desist, saying, "If you make the least damn bit of noise I'll send you to hell!" He then lighted a lamp and went into the steerage. George, becoming rattled at this conduct of his unnatural brother, again took the rattle for the purpose of alarming some one; Comstock arrived in time to prevent him, and with threatenings dark and diabolical, so congealed the blood of his trembling brother, that even had he possessed the power of alarming the unconscious and fated victims below, his life would have been the forfeit of his temerity.

Comstock now laid something heavy upon a small work bench near the cabin gangway, which was afterwards found to be a boarding knife. It is an instrument used by whalers to cut the blubber when hoisting it in, is about four feet in length, two or three inches wide, and necessarily kept very sharp and for greater convenience when in use, is two edged.

The Globe Mutiny.

In giving a detail of this chilling transaction, we shall be guided by the description given of it by the younger Comstock, who, as has been observed, was upon the deck at the time, and afterwards learned several particulars from his brother, to whom alone they could have been known. Comstock went down into the cabin, accompanied by Silas Payne, or Paine, of Sag Harbor, John Oliver, of Shields, Eng., William Humphries (the steward), of Philadelphia, and Thomas Liliston; the latter, however, went no farther than the cabin gangway, and then ran forward and turned in. According to his own story he did not think they would attempt to put their designs in execution, until he saw them actually descending into the cabin, having gone so far, to use his own expression, to show himself as brave as any of them. But we believe he had not the smallest idea of assisting the villains. Comstock entered the cabin so silently as not to be perceived by the man at the helm, who was first apprised of his having begun the work of death, by the sound of a

24

heavy blow with an axe, which he distinctly heard.

The captain was asleep in a hammock, suspended in the cabin, his stateroom being uncomfortably warm; Comstock approaching him with the axe, struck him a blow upon the head, which was nearly severed in two by the first stroke. After repeating the blow, he ran to Payne, who it seems was stationed with the before-mentioned boarding knife to attack the mate, as soon as the captain was killed. At this instant, Payne making a thrust at the mate, he awoke, and terrified, exclaimed, "What! what! what! Is this —— Oh, Payne! Oh, Comstock! Don't kill me, don't; have I not always ——" Here Comstock interrupted him, saying, "Yes! you have always been a d—d rascal; you tell lies of me out of the ship, will you? It's a d—d good time to beg now, but you're too late;" here the mate sprang and grasped him by the throat. In the scuffle, the light which Comstock held in his hand was knocked out, and the axe fell from his hand, but the grasp of Mr. Beetle upon his throat did not prevent him from making Payne understand that his weapon was lost, who felt about until he found it, and having given it to Comstock, he managed to strike Mr. Beetle a blow upon the head, which fractured his skull; when he fell into the pantry where he lay groaning, until despatched by Comstock. The steward held a light at this time, while Oliver put in a blow as often as possible.

The second and third mates, fastened in their staterooms, lay in their berths listening, fearing to speak; and being ignorant of the numerical strength of the mutineers, and unarmed, thought it best to wait the dreadful issue, hoping that their lives might yet be spared.

Comstock, leaving a watch at the second mate's door, went upon deck to light another lamp at the binnacle, it having been again accidentally extinguished. He was there asked by his terrified brother, whose agony of mind we will not attempt to portray, if he intended to hurt Smith, the other boat-steerer. He replied that he did; and inquired where he was. George, fearing Smith would immediately be pursued, said he had not seen him. Comstock then perceiving his brother to be shedding tears, asked sternly, "What are you crying about?" "I am afraid," replied George, "that they will hurt me!" "I will hurt you," said he, "if you talk in that manner!"

But the work of death was not yet finished. Comstock took his light into the cabin, and made preparations for attacking the second and third mates, Mr. Fisher, and Mr. Lumbard. After loading two muskets, he fired one through the door, in the direction, as near as he could judge, of the officers, and then inquired if either was shot. Fisher replied, "Yes, I am shot in the mouth." Previous to his shooting Fisher, Lumbard asked if he was going to kill him. To which he answered with apparent unconcern, "Oh, no, I guess not."

They now opened the door, and Comstock, making a pass at Lumbard, missed him, and fell into the stateroom. Mr. Lumbard collared him,

27

but he escaped from his hands. Mr. Fisher had got the gun, and actually presented the bayonet to the monster's heart. But Comstock assuring him that his life should be spared if he gave it up, he immediately did so, when Comstock immediately ran Mr. Lumbard through the body several times.

He then turned to Mr. Fisher, and told him there was no hope for him. "You have got to die," said he; "remember the scrape you got me into, when in company with the Enterprise, of Nantucket." The "scrape," alluded to was as follows: Comstock came up to Mr. Fisher to wrestle with him; Fisher being the most athletic of the two, handled him with so much ease, that Comstock in a fit of passion struck him. At this Fisher seized him, and laid him upon the deck several times in pretty rough manner.

Comstock then made some violent threats, which Fisher paid no attention to, but which now fell upon his soul with all the horrors of reality. Finding his enemy deaf to his remon-

28

strances, and entreaties, he said, "If there is no hope, I will at least die like a man!" and having by order of Comstock, turned back to, he said in a firm voice, "I am ready!"

Comstock then put the muzzle of the gun to his head, and fired, which instantly put an end to his existence. Mr. Lumbard, during this time, was begging for life, although no doubt mortally wounded. Comstock turned to him and said, "I am a bloody man! I have a bloody hand and will be revenged!" and again ran him through the body with a bayonet. He then begged for a little water; "I'll give you water," said he, and once more plunging the weapon in his body, left him for dead.

Thus it appears that this more than demon murdered with his own hand, all the officers. Gladly would we wash from "memory's waste" all remembrance of that bloody night. The compassionate reader, however, whose heart sickens within him at the perusal, as does ours at the recital of this tale of woe, will not, we hope, disapprove our publishing these melancholy facts to the world. As, through the boundless mercy of Providence, we have been restored to the bosom of our families and homes, we deemed it a duty we owe to the world, to record our "unvarnished tale."

CHAPTER II.

SMITH, the other boat-steerer, who had been marked as one of the victims, on hearing the noise in the cabin, went aft, apprehending an altercation between the captain and some of the other officers, little dreaming that innocent blood was flowing in torrents. But what was his astonishment, when he beheld Comstock brandishing the boarding knife, and heard him exclaim, "I am the bloody man, and will have revenge!" Horror-struck, he hurried forward, and asked the crew in the forecastle, what he should do. Some urged him to secrete himself in the hold, others to go aloft until Comstock's rage should be abated; but alas! the reflection that the ship afforded no secure hiding place, determined him to confront the ringleader, and if he could not save his life by fair means, to sell

31

it dearly. He was soon called for by Comstock, who upon meeting him, threw his bloody arms around his neck, and embracing him, said, "You are going to be with us, are you not?" The reader will discover the good policy of Smith when he unhesitatingly answered, "Oh, yes, I will do anything you require."

All hands were now called to make sail, and at the same time a light was set as a signal for the Lyra to tack; while the Globe was kept upon the same tack, which very soon caused a separation of the two ships. All the reefs were turned out, top-gallant-sails set, and all sail made on the ship, the wind being quite light.

The mutineers then threw the body of the captain overboard, after wantonly piercing his bowels with a boarding knife, which was driven by an axe until the point protruded from his throat. In Mr. Beetle, the mate, the lamp of life had not entirely gone out, but he was committed to the deep.

Orders were next given to have the bodies of Mr. Fisher and Mr. Lumbard brought up.

The Globe Mutiny.

A rope was fastened to Fisher's neck, by which he was hauled upon deck. A rope was made fast to Mr. Lumbard's feet, and in this way was he got upon deck, but when in the act of being thrown from the ship, he caught the plank-shear, and appealed to Comstock, reminding him of his promise to save him, but in vain; for the monster forced him from his hold, and he fell into the sea. As he appeared to be yet capable of swimming, a boat was ordered to be lowered to pursue and finish him, fearing he might be picked up by the Lyra, which order was as soon countermanded as given, Comstock fearing, no doubt, a desertion of his murderous companions.

We will now present the reader with a journal of our passage to the Mulgrave Islands, for which group we shaped our course.

1824, January 26th. At 2 A.M. from being nearly calm a light breeze sprung up, which increased to a fresh breeze by 4 A.M. This day cleaned out the cabin, which was a scene of blood and destruction, of which the recollection at this day chills the blood in our veins. Everything bearing marks of the murder was brought on deck and washed.

Lat. 5° 50′ N., Long. 159° 13′ W.

January 27th. These twenty-four hours commenced with moderate breezes from the eastward. Middle and latter part calm. Employed in cleaning the small arms, which were fifteen in number, and making cartridge boxes.

Lat. 30° 45′ N., Long. 160° 45′ W.

January 28th. This day, experienced fine weather, and light breezes from north by west. The black steward was hung for the following crime:

George Comstock was appointed steward after the mutiny, and business calling him into the cabin, he saw the former steward, now called the purser, engaged in loading a pistol. He asked him what he was doing that for. His reply was, "I have heard something very strange, and I am going to be ready for it." This information was immediately carried to Comstock, who called to Payne, now mate, and bid him follow him.

The Globe Mutiny.

On entering the cabin they saw Humphries still standing with the pistol in his hand. On being demanded what he was going to do with it, he said he had heard something which made him afraid of his life.

Comstock told him if he had heard anything, that he ought to have come to him, and let him know, before he began loading pistols. He then demanded to know what he had heard. Humphries answered at first in a very suspicious and ambiguous manner, but at length said, "that Gilbert Smith, the boat-steerer who was saved, and Peter Kidder, were going to retake the ship." This appeared highly improbable, but they were summoned to attend a council at which Comstock presided, and asked if they had entertained any such intentions. They positively denied ever having had conversation upon the subject. All this took place in the evening. The next morning the parties were summoned, and a jury of two men called. Humphries, under guard of six men, armed with muskets, was arraigned, and Smith and Kidder, seated upon a chest near him. The prisoner was asked a few questions touching his intentions, which he answered, but low and indistinctly. The trial, if it may be so called, had progressed so far, when Comstock made a speech in the following words: "It appears that William Humphries has been accused guilty of a treacherous and base act, in loading a pistol for the purpose of shooting Mr. Payne and myself. Having been tried, the jury will now give in their verdict, whether guilty or not guilty. If guilty he shall be hanged to a studding-sail boom, rigged out eight feet upon the fore-yard, but if found not guilty, Smith and Kidder shall be hung upon the aforementioned gallows." But the doom of Humphries had been sealed the night before, and kept secret from all except the jury, who returned a verdict of guilty. Preparations were immediately made for his execution. His watch was taken from him, and he was then taken forward and seated upon the rail, with a cap drawn over his face, and the rope placed round his neck.

The Globe Mutiny.

Every man was ordered to take hold of the execution rope, to be ready to run him up when Comstock should give the signal, by ringing the bell.

He was now asked if he had anything to say, as he had but fourteen seconds to live. He began by saying, "Little did I think I was born to come to this——" the bell struck, and he was immediately swung to the yard-arm. He died without a struggle, and after he had hung a few minutes, the rope was cut to let him fall overboard, but getting entangled aloft the body was towed some distance alongside, when a runner hook (a large hook used when hoisting in the blubber) was attached to it, to sink it, when the rope was again cut and the body disappeared. His chest was now overhauled, and sixteen dollars in specie was found, which he had taken from the captain's trunk. Thus ended the life of one of the mutineers, while the blood of innocent victims was scarcely washed from his hands, much less the guilty stain from his soul.

The Globe Mutiny.

February 7th. These twenty-four hours commenced with thick, squally weather. Middle part clear and fine weather. Hove to at 2 A.M. and at 6 made sail, and steered west by south. At half past eight, made an island ahead, one of the Kingsmill group. Stood in with the land and received a number of canoes alongside, the natives, however, having nothing to sell us but a few beads of their own manufacture. We saw some cocoanut and other trees upon the shore, and discovered many of the natives upon the beach and some dogs. The principal food of these islanders is a kind of bread fruit, which they pound very fine and mix with fish.

February 8th. Commences squally with fresh breezes from the northward. Took a departure from Kingsmill Island, one of the group of that name; in lat. 1° 27' N., and long. 175° 14' E. In the morning passed through the channel between Marshall's and Gilbert's Islands; luffed to and dispatched a boat to Marshall's Island, but did not land, as the natives appeared hostile, and those who swam off to the boat, endeavored to steal from her. When about to leave, a volley of musketry was discharged at them, which probably killed or wounded some of them. The boat then gave chase to a canoe, paddled by two of the natives, which were fired upon when within gunshot, when they immediately ceased paddling; and on the boat approaching them, discovered that one of the natives was wounded. In the most supplicating manner they held up a jacket, manufactured from a kind of flag, and some beads, being all they possessed, giving their inhuman pursuers to understand that all should be theirs if they would spare their lives. The wounded native laid down in the bottom of the boat, and from his convulsed frame and trembling lip, no doubt remained but that the wound was mortal. The boat returned on board, and we made sail for the Mulgrave Islands. Here was another sacrifice; an innocent child of nature shot down, merely to gratify the most wanton and unprovoked cruelty which could possibly possess the heart of man. The unpolished savage, a stranger to the more tender sympathies of the human heart, which are cultivated and enjoyed by civilized nations, nurtures in his bosom a flame of revenge, which only the blood of those who have injured him, can damp; and when years have rolled away, this act of cruelty will be remembered by these islanders, and made the pretext to slaughter every white man who may fall into their hands.

February 11th. Commenced with strong breezes from the northward. At half past meridian made the land bearing east, northeast four leagues ahead. Stood in and received a number of canoes alongside. Sent a boat on shore, and brought off a number of women, a large quantity of cocoanuts, and some fish. Stood off shore most of the night, and February 12th, in the morning stood in shore again and landed the women. We then stood along shore looking out for an anchorage, and reconnoitering the country, in the hope of finding some spot suitable for cultivation; but in this we were disappointed, or more properly speaking, they, the mutineers; for we had no will of our own, while our bosoms were torn with the most conflicting passions, in which hope and despair alternately gained the ascendency.

February 13th. After having stood off all night, we in the morning stood in, and after coasting the shores of several small islands, we came to one, low and narrow, where it was determined the ship should be anchored. When nearly ready to let go, a man was sent into the chains to sound, who pronounced twelve fathoms; but at the next cast, could not get bottom. We continued to stand in, until we got regular sounding, and anchored within five rods of the shore, on a coral rock bottom, in seven fathoms water. Then the ship was moored with a kedge astern, sails furled, and all hands retired to rest, except an anchor watch.

February 14th, was spent in looking for a landing place. In the morning a boat was sent to the eastward, but returned with the information that no good landing-place could be found, the shore being very rocky. At 2 P.M. she was sent in an opposite direction, but returned at night without having met with better success; when it was determined to land at the place where we lay; notwithstanding it was very rocky. Nothing of consequence was done, until Sunday, February 15, 1824, when all hands were set to work to construct a raft out of the spare spars, upon which to convey the provisions, etc., on shore.

The laws by which we were now governed had been made by Comstock, soon after the mutiny, and read as follows:

"That if any one saw a sail and did not report it immediately, he should be put to death. If any one refused to fight a ship he should be put to death; and the manner of their death, this: They shall be bound hand and foot and boiled in the try pots of boiling oil." Every man was made to seal and sign this instrument, the seals of the mutineers being black, and the remainder, blue and white. The raft or stage being completed, it was anchored, so that one end rested upon the rocks, the other being kept seaward by the anchor. During the first day many articles were brought from the ship in boats to the raft, and from thence conveyed on shore. Another raft was made, however, by laying spars upon two boats, and boards again upon them, which at high water would float well up on the shore. The following, as near as can be recollected, were the articles landed from the ship (and the intention was, when all should have been got on shore, to haul the ship on shore, or, as near as possible and burn her). One mainsail, one foresail, one mizzen-topsail, one spanker, one driver, one main-topgallant sail, two lower studding sails, two royals, two topmast studding sails, two topgallant studding sails, one mizzen staysail, two mizzen topgallant sails, one fly-jib (thrown overboard, being a little torn), three boats' sails (new), three or four casks of bread, eight or ten barrels of flour, forty barrels of beef and pork, three or more 60-gallon casks of molasses, one and a half barrels of sugar, one barrel of dried apples, one cask of vinegar, two casks of rum, one or two barrels domestic coffee, one keg W. I. coffee, one and a half chests of tea, one barrel of pickles, one barrel cranberries, one box chocolate, one cask of towlines, three or more coils of cordage, one coil rattling, one coil lance warp, ten or fifteen balls spun yarn, one ball worming, one stream cable, one larboard lower anchor, all the spare spars, every chest of clothing, most of the ship's tools, etc., etc. The ship by this time was considerably unrigged.

On the following day, Monday, February 16th, Payne, the second in the mutiny, who was on the ship attending to the discharge of articles from her, sent word to Comstock, who with Gilbert Smith, and a number of the crew were on shore, attending to the landing of the raft, "that if he did not act differently with regard to the plunder, such as making presents to the natives of the officers' fine clothing, etc., he would do no more, but quit the ship and come on shore." Comstock had been very liberal to the natives in this way, and his object was, no doubt, to attach them as much as possible to his person, as it must have been suggested to his guilty mind, that however he himself might have become a misanthrope, yet there were those around him whose souls shuddered at the idea of being forever exiled from their country and friends, whose hands were yet unstained by blood, but who might yet imbrue them, for the purpose of escape from lonely exile, and cruel tyranny.

When the foregoing message was received from Payne, Comstock commanded his presence immediately on shore, and interrogated him as to what he meant by sending such a message. After considerable altercation, which took place in the tent, Comstock was heard to say, "I helped to take the ship, and have navigated her to this place. I have also done all I could to get the sails and rigging on shore, and now you may do what you please with her; but if any man wants anything of me, I'll take a musket with him!"

The Globe Mutiny.

"That is what I want," replied Payne, "and I am ready!" This was a check upon the murderer, who had now the offer of becoming a duellist; and he only answered by saying, "I will go on board once more, and then you may do as you please."

He then went on board, and after destroying the paper upon which were recorded the "Laws," returned, went into the tent with Payne, and putting a sword into a scabbard, exclaimed "This shall stand by me as long as I live."

We ought not to omit to mention that during the time he was on board the ship, he challenged the persons there to fight him, and as he was leaving, exclaimed: "I am going to leave you; look out for yourselves!"

After obtaining from Payne, permission to carry with him a cutlass, a knife, and some hooks and lines, he took his departure, and as was afterwards ascertained, immediately joined a gang of natives, and endeavored to incite them to slay Payne and his companions. At dusk of this day he passed the tent, accompanied by about fifty of the natives, in the direction of their village, upwards of a league distant. Payne came on board, and after expressing apprehensions that Comstock would persuade the natives to kill us all, picked out a number of the crew to go on shore for the night, and stationed sentinels around the tent, with orders to shoot any one who should attempt to approach without giving the countersign. The night, however, passed without any one appearing; but early on the morning of the 17th of February, Comstock was discovered at some distance coming toward the tent. It had been before proposed to Smith by Payne, to shoot him; but poor Smith, like ourselves, dare do no other than remain upon the side of neutrality.

Oliver, whom the reader will recollect as one of the poor wretches concerned in the mutiny, hurried on shore, and with Payne and others, made preparations to put him to death. After loading a number of muskets they stationed themselves in front of the tent, and waited his

47

approach. A bushy spot of ground intervening, he did not make his appearance until within a short distance of the tent, which, as soon as he saw, he drew his sword and walked quickly towards it in a menacing manner; but as soon as he saw a number of the muskets levelled at him, he waved his hand, and cried out, "Don't shoot me, don't shoot me! I will not hurt you!" At this moment they fired and he fell. Payne, fearing he might pretend to be shot, ran to him with an axe, and nearly severed his head from his body. There were four muskets fired at him, but only two balls took effect. One entered his right breast, and passed out near his backbone, the other through his head.

Thus ended the life of perhaps as cruel, blood-thirsty and vindictive a being as ever bore the form of humanity.

All hands were now called to attend his burial, which was conducted in the same inconsistent manner which had marked the proceedings of the actors in this tragedy. While some were engaged in sewing the body in a piece of canvas, others were employed in digging a grave in the sand, adjacent to the place of his decease, which, by order of Payne, was made five feet deep. Every article attached to him, including his cutlass, was buried with him, except his watch; and the ceremonies consisted in reading a chapter from the Bible over him, and firing a musket.

Only twenty-two days had elapsed after the perpetration of the massacre on board the ship, when with all his sins upon his head, he was hurried into eternity.

No duty was done during the remainder of the day, except the selection by Payne, of six men, to go on board the ship and take charge of her, under command of Smith, who had communicated his intentions to a number, of running away with the ship. We think we cannot do better than to give an account of their escape in the words of Smith himself. It may be well to remark, that Payne had ordered the two binnacle compasses to be brought on shore, they being the only ones left on board, except a hanging compass suspended in the cabin. Secreting one of the binnacle compasses, he took the hanging compass on shore, and the exchange was not discovered.

"At 7 P.M. we began to make preparations for our escape with the ship. I went below to prepare some weapons for our defence should we be attacked by Payne, while the others, as silently as possible, were employed in clearing the running rigging, for everything was in the utmost confusion. Having found one musket, three bayonets, and some whale lances, they were laid handy, to prevent the ship being boarded. A handsaw well greased was laid upon the windlass to saw off the cable, and the only remaining hatchet on board was placed by the mizzenmast, to cut the stern moorings when the ship should have sufficiently swung off. Taking one man with me, we went upon the fore-topsail-yard, loosed the sail and turned out the reefs, while two others were loosing the main-topsail, and mainsail. I will not insult the reader's good sense by assuring him that this was a duty, upon the success of which seemed to hang our very existence. By this time, the moon was rising, which rendered it dangerous to delay, for those who had formed a resolution to swim on board, and accompany us. The bunts of the sails being yet confined aloft, by their respective gaskets, I sent a man on the foreyard and another upon the fore-topsail-yard, with orders to let fall, when I should give the word; one man being at the helm, and two others at the fore tack.

"It was now half past nine o'clock, when I took the handsaw, and in less than two minutes the cable was off. The ship paid off very quickly, and when her head was off the land, there being a breeze from that quarter, the hawser was cut and all the sail we could make upon the ship immediately set, a fine fair wind blowing. A raft of iron hoops, which was towing alongside, was cut adrift, and we congratulated each other upon our fortunate escape, for even with a vast extent of ocean to traverse, hope excited in our bosoms a belief that we should again embrace our friends, and our joy was heightened by the reflection that we might be the means of rescuing the innocents left behind, and having the guilty punished."

After a long and boisterous passage the ship arrived at Valparaiso, when she was taken possession of by the American Consul, Michael Hogan, Esq., and the persons on board were put in irons on board a French frigate, there being no American man-of-war in port. Their names were, Gilbert Smith, George Comstock, Stephen Kidder, Joseph Thomas, Peter C. Kidder, and Anthony Hanson.

Subsequently they were all examined before the United States Consul; and with the following, an examination of Gilbert Smith, we shall commence another chapter.

CHAPTER III.

UNITED STATES CONSULATE.

VALPARAISO, June 15, 1824.

GILBERT SMITH examined on oath, touching the mutiny and murder on board the whale ship Globe, of Nantucket, Massachusetts, in the Pacific Ocean.

Question. Who were the captain and mates of the ship Globe?

Answer. Thomas Worth, captain; William Beetle, first mate; John Lumbard, second mate; Nathaniel Fisher, third mate.

Q. Where were you born?

A. In the town of Edgartown, State of Massachusetts.

Q. Did you sail from thence in the ship Globe, of Nantucket, December 20, 1822, and in what capacity?

A. Yes; as a boat-steerer.

Q. Was there anything like mutiny on board the ship during her passage to the Sandwich Islands?

53

The Globe Mutiny.

A. No.

Q. How many men belonged to the ship on sailing from Nantucket?

A. Twenty-one in all.

Q. Did any run away at the Sandwich Islands?

A. Six men ran away and one was discharged.

Q. How many men were shipped in their places?

A. John Oliver, of Shields, England; Silas Payne, of Rhode Island; Thomas Liliston, of Virginia; William Humphries, of Philadelphia (black); Anthony Hanson, of Barnstable; and a native of the Sandwich Islands.

Q. On what day or night did this murderous mutiny take place?

A. On Sunday night, the 26th of January, this year; in the morning of that day there was a great disturbance, in consequence of Joseph Thomas having insulted the captain, for which he was whipped by the captain, with the end of the main buntline. The part of the crew not stationed stood in the hatchway during the punishment.

Q. Did anything in consequence happen, during that day?

The Globe Mutiny.

A. No; I lived aft; I heard nothing about it; Captain Joy, of the Lyra, was on board nearly all day.

Q. How were you stationed during the night?

A. The captain, first and second mates, kept no watch during that night; the rest of the crew were stationed in three watches, in charge of the third mate and boat steerers.

Q. Who had charge of the first watch during that night?

A. I had charge of the watch from 7 to 10 o'clock. At 8 the captain came on deck, and had two reefs taken in the topsails, and at 9 went down, leaving me the orders for the night, to keep the ship by the wind, until 2 o'clock, and not to tack until the other watch came up; and on tacking, a light to be set for the Lyra, which was in company, to tack also.

At 10 o'clock I went below, being relieved by the boat-steerer Comstock, to whom I passed the orders given me by the captain. (Here follows a detailed account of the mutiny, with which the reader has already been made acquainted.)

Q. Do you believe that Joseph Thomas had

any knowledge of Comstock's intent to commit murder that night?

A. I think he must have known something about it, according to his talk.

Q. Do you believe that any other person in the ship, besides those persons who committed the murder, knew of the intention?

A. Thomas Liliston knew abot it, because he went to the cabin door with an axe, and a boat knife in his hand, in company with the murderers, but he did not go below.

Q. Did you live with them aft, afterwards?

A. No; I lived in the forecastle, but all on board ate in the cabin.

Q. Name all the persons you left on the Island, where you cut the cable of the ship and escaped?

A. Silas Payne, John Oliver (being the principal mutineers next to Samuel B. Comstock), Thomas Liliston, Rowland Coffin, William Lay, Cyrus M. Hussey, Columbus Worth, and the Sandwich Island native, called Joseph Brown. The last five I believe ignorant of any knowledge of the intent to murder.

Q. What became of Samuel B. Comstock,

who was the head mutineer, after he landed upon the island?

A. He was shot on the morning of the 17th of February, by Silas Payne, and John Oliver, his associates in all the mutiny and murderous course they had pursued, and buried five feet deep on the beach near their tent; a chapter was read from the Bible by me, acting under the orders of Payne, and muskets were fired by his orders, by the men.

Q. Why did they murder Comstock?

A. For giving away to the natives clothes and other articles before they were divided.

Q. Were the natives friendly and quiet?

A. Yes; very peaceable; gave away anything they had; bread fruit, cocoanuts and other things.

Q. How did Joseph Thomas conduct himself during the passage from the Isle to this port?

A. In common, when help was called, he was the first man disobedient, and frequently said he would do as he pleased.

Q. Did he often speak of the murder, or of his knowledge of it about to take place?

A. I only remember having heard him twice. I told him when we arrived, I would inform the

American Consul of it; and he replied, he should own all he knew about it.

Q. To what State does he belong, to your knowledge?

A. To the State of Connecticut, he says.

(Signed.) GILBERT SMITH.

Sworn to, before me at Valparaiso, this eighteenth day of June, 1824.

(Signed.) MICHAEL HOGAN,
United States Consul.

The examination of the others who came in the ship was but a repetition of the foregoing. All, however, concurred in believing that Joseph Thomas was privy to the intention to mutiny and murder the officers.

The ship was then furnished with necessary sails and rigging, and placed in charge of a Captain King, who brought her to the Island of Nantucket, arriving on Sunday, November 21, 1824. Another examination was held before Josiah Hussey, Esq., and all testified as before the American Consul, at Valparaiso.

Thomas, who was kept in irons as soon as

land was discovered, was arraigned before the above-named justice and after an elaborate hearing, the prisoner was committed to jail, to take his trial at the following term of the U. S. District Court, and the witnesses recognized in the sum of three hundred dollars each.

Leaving Thomas awaiting his trial, and the others in the enjoyment of the society of their families and friends, we will return to the Mulgrave Islands, the scene of no inconsiderable portion of our distresses and adventures.

On the 17th of February, when night came, the watch was set, consisting of two men, whose duty it was to guard against the thefts of the natives. At about 10 P.M., all hands were awakened by the cry: "The ship has gone, the ship has gone!" Every one hastened to the beach and verified the truth of the report for themselves. Some who were ignorant of the intention of Smith and others to take the ship, were of the opinion that the strong breeze then blowing, had caused her to drag her anchor, and that she would return in the morning.

The Globe Mutiny.

The morning came, but nothing was to be seen upon the broad expanse of ocean, save here and there a solitary sea gull, perched upon the crested billows. Payne, in a paroxysm of rage, vented the most dreadful imprecations; swearing that could he get them once more in his power, he would put them to instant death. Not so with us; a ray of hope shot through our minds, that this circumstance might be the means of rescuing us from our lonely situation. The writers of this narrative were upon the most intimate terms, and frequently, though carefully, sympathized with each other upon their forlorn situation. We dare not communicate our disaffection of the government of the two surviving mutineers, Payne and Oliver, to the others, fearing they might not agree with us in opinion, and we had too good reason to believe that there was one, who, although unstained by blood, yet from his conduct, seemed to sanction the proceedings of the mutineers.

The natives assembled in great numbers around the tent, expressing great surprise at the ship's having left, Payne giving them to understand that the wind had forced her to sea, and that from her want of sails, rigging, etc., she must be lost, and would never return. The natives received the assurance with satisfaction, but it was evident Payne apprehended her safe arrival at some port, and his own punishment; for we immediately set to work to tear one boat to pieces, for the purpose of raising upon another, which was to have a deck; Payne alleging as a reason for this, that the natives might compel us to leave the island. We leave the reader to judge, however, of his motives, while we proceed to give an account of what actually did transpire.

The natives in considerable numbers continued to attend us, and while the work was progressing, exhibited a great deal of curiosity. Their deportment towards us continued to be of the most friendly nature, continuing to barter with us, giving us bread fruit, cocoanuts, etc., for which they received in return pieces of iron

hoop, nails, and such articles as we could con-
veniently spare.

The small islands of this group are frequently
only separated by what are sometimes denomi-
nated causeways, or in other words, connected
by reefs of coral extending from the extreme
point of one island and connecting it with
another. These reefs are nearly dry at low
water, and the communication is easily kept up
between them by the natives on foot.

On the 19th, in the morning, having obtained
permission, several of us left the tent, travelling
to the eastward. After crossing upon the causeways to several adjacent islands, we discovered
numerous tracks of the natives in the sand, and
having followed them about seven miles, came to
a village consisting of about twenty or thirty
families; and were received by them with great
hospitality. They presented us with bread fruit,
and the milk of cocoanuts, while the wonder
and astonishment of those who had not as yet
seen us, particularly the women and children,
were expressed by the most uncouth grimaces,

attended with boisterous laughter, and capering around us. What more particularly excited their astonishment, was the whiteness of our skins, and their mirth knew no bounds when they heard us converse.

Early on the morning of the 20th we were ordered to go to work upon the boat; but at the request of a number, this duty was dispensed with, and we were permitted to stroll about the island. A number went to the village, carrying with them muskets, at the report of which and the effect produced by the balls, the natives were struck with wonder and astonishment. The reader will no doubt agree with us when we pronounce this to have been a bad policy, for they certainly disliked to have visitors possessed of such formidable and destructive weapons. They, however, continued to visit the tent without our discovering any hostile intentions, and we continued to put the utmost confidence in them, or more properly speaking to live without any fear of them.

I (William Lay) left the tent on a visit to the

village, where I was received with the same kindness as before. An old man between fifty and sixty years of age, pressed me to go to his house and tarry during the night, which I did. The natives continued in and around the tent until a late hour, gratifying their curiosity by a sight of me. I was provided with some mats to sleep upon; but the rats, with which the island abounds, prevented my enjoying much sleep.

At 10 o'clock I took my leave of them, with the exception of a number, who accompanied me to the tent.

Silas Payne and John Oliver, together with two or three others, set out in one of the boats, for the purpose of exploring the island, and making new discoveries, leaving the rest of us to guard the tent. They were absent but one night, when they returned, bringing with them two young women, whom Payne and Oilver took as their wives. The women apparently showed no dissatisfaction, but on the contrary appeared much diverted. Payne now put such confidence in the natives that he dispensed with having a watch kept during the night, and slept as secure as though he had been in his native country.

Payne, on awaking near morning, found the woman that he had brought to live with him was missing. After searching the tent and finding nothing of her, he concluded she had fled. He accordingly armed himself, together with John Oliver, and Thomas Lilliston (with muskets), and set out for the nearest village, for the purpose of searching her out. They arrived at the village before it was light, and secreted themselves near an Indian hut, where they awaited the approach of day, in hopes of seeing her. Accordingly, at the approach of daylight, they discovered the hut literally thronged with natives, and among the number, they discovered the woman they were in search of. At this moment one of our men fired a blank cartridge over their heads, and then presented themselves to their view, which frightened the natives in such a manner that they left the hut and fled. Payne then pursued after, firing over their heads, until he caught the one he was after, and then left the village for his own tent. On arriving at the tent, he took her, gave her a severe flogging, and then put her in irons, and carried on in this kind of style until he was killed by them, and called to render up his accounts to his offended Judge.

This severity on the part of Payne irritated the natives, and was undoubtedly the cause of their committing depredations and theft, and finally murdering all our remaining crew, excepting myself and Hussey.

Early on the succeeding morning it was discovered that the tool chest had been broken open, and a hatchet, chisel, and some other articles purloined by the natives. Payne worked himself into a passion, and said he would be revenged. During the day he informed a number of the natives of what had been done (who signified much regret at the circumstances), and vowing vengeance if the articles were not returned. During this day the natives frequented the tent more than they had ever done before;

and at night one of them came running with one half of the chisel which had been stolen, it having been broken in two.

Payne told them it was but half of what he required, and put the Indian in irons, signifying to him, that in the morning he must go with him to the village, and produce the rest of the articles, and also point out the persons engaged in breaking open the chest. The poor native seemed much chagrined at his confinement; yet his companions, who remained near the tent during the night, manifested no dissatisfaction, which we could observe.

In the morning, Payne selected four men, viz.: Rowland Coffin, Rowland Jones, Cyrus M. Hussey, and Thomas Liliston, giving them each a musket, some powder and fine shot; declining to give them balls, saying, the report of the muskets would be sufficient to intimidate them. The prisoner was placed in charge of these men, who had orders to go to the village, and recover the hatchet, and bring back the person whom the prisoner might point out as the thief.

They succeeded in getting the hatchet, but when about to return, the natives in a great body attacked them with stones. Finding that they retreated, the natives pursued them, and having overtaken Rowland Jones, killed him upon the spot. The remainder, although bruised with the stones which these islanders had thrown with great precision, arrived at the tent with the alarming intelligence of the difficulty;—while the natives followed in the rear armed for war.

No time was lost in arming ourselves, while the natives, collected from all quarters, and at a short distance from the tent, seemed to hold a kind of council. After deliberating some time, they began to tear to pieces one of the boats.

These were of vital importance to our guilty commander, and he ventured to go to them for the purpose of pacifying them. One of the chiefs sat down upon the ground with him, and after they had sat a few moments, Payne accompanied the chief into the midst of the natives. After a conference with them which lasted nearly an hour, he returned to the tent, saying that he had pacified the natives upon the following conditions. They were to have every article belonging to us, even to the tent; and Payne had assured them of his willingness, and of that of the others to live with, and be governed by them, and to adopt their mode of living. We have reason to doubt the sincerity of Payne in this respect, for what was to us a hope, which we cherished with peculiar pleasure, must have been to him, a source of fearful anticipation— we mean the probable safe arrival of the ship in the United States, which should result in our deliverance. Our situation at this time was truly alarming; and may we not with propriety say, distressing? Surrounded by a horde of savages, brandishing their war clubs and javelins, our more savage commanders (Payne and Oliver), in anxious suspense as to the result of their negotiations with them; no refuge from either foe, and what contributed not a little to our unhappiness, was a consciousness of being innocent of having in the least manner wilfully aided the destroyers of the lives of our officers, and the authors of our now, truly unhappy situation.

The natives now began to help themselves to whatever articles suited them, and when some of them began to pull the tent down, an old man and his wife took hold of me, and after conducting me a few rods from the tent, sat down, keeping fast hold of my hands. Under the most fearful apprehensions I endeavored to get away from them, but they insisted on detaining me. I endeavored to console myself with the idea, that gratitude had prompted them to take care of me, as I had frequently taken the part of this old woman, when she had been teased by others; but alas! the reflection followed, that if this was the case, there was a probability that not only my bosom friend was about to be sacrificed, but I should be left alone to drag out a weary existence, with beings, strangers to the endearing ties which bind the hearts of civilized men.

The Globe Mutiny.

Whether Payne and his associates offered any resistance to the course now pursued by the natives or not, I do not know. Suffice it to say, that all at once my ears were astounded with the most terrifying whoops and yells; then a massacre commenced, but little exceeded by the one perpetrated on board the Globe. Our men fled in all directions, but met a foe at every turn. Liliston and Joe Brown (the Sandwich Islander) fell within six feet of me, and as soon as down, the natives macerated their heads with large stones. The first whom I saw killed, was Columbus Worth. An old woman, apparently sixty years of age, ran him through with a spear, and finished him with stones.

My protectors, for now they were truly so, shut out the scene by laying down upon the top of me, to hide me from the view of the merciless foe. I was however discovered, and one of the natives attempted to get a blow at me with a handspike, which was prevented by them; when, after a few words, he hurried away.

As soon as the work of death had been completed, the old man took me by the hand and hurried me along toward the village. My feet were very much lacerated in passing over the causeways of sharp coral rock, but my conductor, fearing we might be pursued, hurried me onward to the village, where we arrived about noon. In a few minutes the wigwam or hut of the old man, was surrounded, and all seeming to talk at once, and with great excitement, I anticipated death at every moment. Believing myself the sole survivor, the reader must pardon any attempt to describe my feelings when I saw a number of the natives approaching the hut, and in the midst, Cyrus M. Hussey, conducted with great apparent kindness.

Notwithstanding we had both been preserved much after the same manner, we could not divest ourselves of the apprehension, that perhaps we had been preserved for a short time, to suffer some lingering death.

Our interview was only long enough to satisfy each other that we alone survived the massacre,

The Globe Mutiny.

when we were separated; Hussey being taken
away, and it seemed quite uncertain, even if our
lives were spared, whether we ever saw each other
again.

CHAPTER IV.

On the following day, however, accompanied by natives, we met at the scene of destruction, and truly it was an appalling one to us. The mangled corpses of our companions, rendered more ghastly from the numerous wounds they had received, the provisions, clothing, etc., scattered about the ground, the hideous yells of exultation uttered by the natives, all conspired to render our situation superlatively miserable.

We asked, and obtained leave from our masters, to bury the bodies which lay scattered about. We dug some graves in the sand, and after finishing this melancholy duty, were directed to launch the canoes, preparatory to our departure (for we had come in canoes), when we begged permission, which was readily granted, to take some flour, bread, and pork, and our respective masters assisted us in getting a small quantity of these articles into the largest canoe. We also took a blanket each, some shoes, a number of books, including a Bible, and soon arrived at the landing place near the village. As the natives seemed desirous of keeping us apart, we dare not make any inquiries for each other, but at my request, having boiled some pork in a large shell, Hussey was sent for, and we had a meal together; during which time, the natives assembled in great numbers, all anxious to get a sight, not only of our novel mode of cutting the meat and eating it, but of the manner in which we prepared it. One of them brought us some water in a tin cup, as they had seen us drink frequently when eating.

The natives now began to arrive from distant parts of the islands, many of whom had not yet heard of us, and we were continually subjected to the examination of men, women and children. The singular color of our skin, was the greatest source of their admiration, and we were frequently importuned to adopt their dress.

The Globe Mutiny.

On the 28th of February, early in the morning the whole village appeared to be in motion. All the adults commenced ornamenting themselves, which to me appeared to render them hideous. After greasing themselves with cocoanut oil, and hanging about them numerous strings of beads, they set off, taking us with them, to a flat piece of ground, about half a mile distant, where we found collected a great number, and all ornamented in the same fantastic manner. Knowing that many of the natives inhabiting islands in the Pacific Ocean are cannibals, we were not without fear that we had been preserved to grace a feast. Our apprehensions, however, were dissipated when we saw them commence a dance, of which we will endeavor to give the reader some idea. The only musical instrument we saw, was a rude kind of drum; and the choristers were all females, say twenty or thirty, each having one of these drums. The music commenced with the women, who began upon a very low key, gradually raising the notes, while the natives accompanied them with the most uncouth gesticulations and grimaces. The precision with which about three hundred of these people, all dancing at a time, regulated their movements, was truly astonishing; while the yelling of the whole body, each trying to exceed the other, rendered the scene to us, not only novel, but terrific.

The dance ended near night, and those natives who lived in a distant part of the island, after gratifying their curiosity by gazing upon us, and even feeling of our skins, took their departure.

After our return to the village, we cooked some meat upon the coals, and with some bread, made a hearty meal. One source of regret to us, was, that the natives began to like our bread, which, heretofore, they had scarcely dared to taste; and particularly the woman whom I called mistress, ate, to use a sea phrase, her full allowance.

The natives expressed great dislike at our conversing together, and prohibited our reading, as much as possible. We never could make them comprehend that the book conveyed ideas to us, expressed in our own language.

Whether from a fear that we might concoct some plan of escape, or that we might be the means of doing them some injury while together, we know not; but about the 1st of April, we discovered that we were about to be separated. The reader may form some idea of our feelings when we were informed that Hussey was to be taken by his master and family, to a distant part of the island. Not having as yet become sufficiently acquainted with their language, we were unable to comprehend the distance from our present location.

It now becomes expedient to present the reader with our separate accounts, in which we hope to be able to convey an idea of the manners and customs of these people. We had experienced in a very short time so many vicissitudes, and passed through so many scenes of distress, that no opportunity was afforded to keep a journal, and notwithstanding, we had even lost the day of the week and month, yet with such force were

The Globe Mutiny.

the principal incidents which ocurred during our exile, impressed upon our minds, that we can with confidence proceed with our narrative, and will commence the next chapter with an account of the adventures of William Lay.

CHAPTER V.

EARLY in the morning of the day on which Hussey left me, preparations were made for his embarkation with his new master and family. We were allowed a short interview, and after taking an affectionate leave of each other, we parted with heavy hearts. The tender ties which bound me to my companion in misfortune, seemed now about to be forever broken asunder. No features to gaze upon but those of my savage masters, and no one with whom I could hold converse, my heart seemed bursting with grief at my lonely situation. On the departure of my companion, the "star of hope," which had often gleamed brightly 'mid the night of our miseries, seemed now about to set forever. After watching the canoe which bore him from me, until she was hid from my view in the distance, I returned to the hut with my master, and as I had eaten

80

but little during the day, the calls of nature induced me to broil my last morsel of meat, with
which, and some bread, I made a tolerable supper. The natives began to be very fond of the
bread, and ate of it as long as it lasted, which un-
fortunately for me, was but a short time.

I informed 'my master that I should like to
have some more of the meat from the place
where the ship had lain. On the following
morning, my master, mistress, and four or five
others, embarked in a canoe, to assist me in procuring some provisions. Observing that they
carried with them a number of clubs, and each a
spear, I was apprehensive of some design upon
my own person; but happily, was soon relieved,
by seeing them wade round a shoal of fish, and
after having frightened them into shoal water,
kill a number with their spears. We then proceeded on, and when we arrived at the tent, they
cooked them after the following manner. A
large fire was kindled, and after the wood was
burned to coals, the fish were thrown on and
snatched and eaten as fast as cooked; although

they were kind enough to preserve a share for me yet the scene around me, prevented my enjoying with them, their meal. The tent which had been torn down, had contained about forty barrels of beef and pork, two hogsheads of molasses, barrels of pickles, all the clothing and stores belonging to the ship, in short, everything valuable, such as charts, nautical instruments, etc., etc. The latter had been broken and destroyed, to make ornaments, while the beef, pork, molasses, and small stores lay scattered promiscuously around. They appeared to set no value on the clothing, except to tear and destroy it. The pieces of beef and pork, from the barrels (which had been all stored), were scattered in every direction, and putrifying in the sun. After putting into the canoes some pork, and a few articles of clothing, we commenced our return; but a strong head wind blowing, we had considerable difficulty in getting back.

For some considerable time, nothing material occurred, and I led as monotonous and lonely a life, as could well be imagined. It is true I was surrounded by fellow-beings; and had all hope of ever seeing my country and friends again been blasted, it is probable I might have been more reconciled to my condition, but I very much doubt if ever perfectly so, as long as reason and reflection held their empire over my mind. My books having been destroyed from a superstitious notion of their possessing some supernatural power, I was left to brood over my situation un-pitied, and alone.

Some time in July, as I judged, Luckiair, son-in-law to my master, Ludjuan, came from a dis-tant part of the group, on a visit, and during the week he remained with us, we became much at-tached to each other. When he told me, that on his return he should pass near the place where Hussey lived, my anxiety to accompany him thus far was so great, that after much persuasion, Ludjuan gave his consent for me to go. On our way we stopped at the tent, and I procured for the last time, a small quantity of the ship's pro-visions, although the meat was some of it in a very decayed state,

The Globe Mutiny.

In consequence of head winds, we were compelled to stop for the night upon a small island, where we found an uninhabited hut; and after cooking some meat, and baking some wet flour, (for it was no other), in the ashes, we took our mats into the hut, and remained until the next day. The wind continuing to blow fresh ahead, we gathered some green bread fruit, and cooked some meat, in the same manner as they cook the largest of their fish, which is this: a hole is dug in the ground, and after it has been filled with wood, it is set on fire, and then covered with stones. As the wood burns away, the heated stones fall to the bottom, which when the fire is out, are covered with a thick layer of green leaves, and then the meat or fish is placed upon these leaves, and covered again in a careful and ingenious manner, and the whole covered with earth. This preserves the juices of the fish, and in this way do they cook most of their fish, with hot stones.

In the afternoon the weather proving more favorable, we left our encampment, and at sundown arrived at a place called Tuckawoa; at which place we were treated with the greatest hospitality. When about to leave, we were presented with bread fruit and cocoanuts in abundance. As we approached the place of Hussey's residence, I discovered him standing on the beach. Our joy at meeting, I will not attempt to describe. We had a short time, however, allowed us, in which to relate our adventures, and condole with each other; for in an hour we were once more separated; and we pursued our course for the residence of Luckiair. After encamping another night upon the beach, we at length arrived at the house of my conductor, which was at a place called Dillybun. His family consisted of a wife and one child, whom we found busily engaged in making a fishing net. When near night, Luckiair and myself went out and gathered some bread fruit, and after making a hearty meal, we slept soundly upon our mats until morning.

A little before noon on the following day, two natives and their wives arrived from Lujnonewort, the place where Hussey lived, and brought me some flour and a piece of meat. The natives would eat of the bread, but would not taste of the meat. I remained here about a week, until Ludjuan came for me. Nothing occurred of note, during our passage back to Milly (the place of my residence); where I was welcomed by the natives with every demonstration of joy. I was sent for by one of the chiefs, who asked many questions, and as a mark of his friendship for me, when I was about to return, presented me with a kind of food called chakaka. My present consisted of a piece about two feet long and six inches in diameter. It is made of a kind of fruit common among these islands, and called by the inhabitants, bup. The fruit is scraped fine, and then laid in the sun until perfectly dry. Some of the leaves of the tree bearing the fruit, are then wrapped round a piece of wood, which is the mould or former, and when securely tied with strings, the former is withdrawn, and into this cylinder of leaves is put the bup, which is of a sweet and pleasant taste.

The Globe Mutiny.

At the urgent request of the natives I now adopted their dress. Having but one pair of trousers and a shirt left, I laid them by for bad weather, and put on the costume of a Mulgrave Islander. This dress, if it may be so called, consists in a broad belt fastened round the waist, from which are suspended two broad tassels. The belt is made from the leaves of the bup tree, and very ingeniously braided, to which are attached the tassels, which are made of a coarser material, being the bark of a small vine, in their language called aht-aht. When the dress is worn, one of the tassels hangs before and the other behind. The sun, as I expected, burned my skin very much; which the natives could not account for, as nothing of the kind ever happened among themselves.

One day there was seen approaching a number of canoes, which we found were loaded with fish for the chiefs, and to my great joy, Hussey was one of the passengers. My master accompanied me to see him; and we anticipated at least a mental feast in each other's society. But of this enjoyment we were deprived by the natives, who were always uneasy when we were conversing together.

I learned, however, from Hussey, that the natives had been kind to him; but before we had an opportunity to communicate to each other our hopes and fears, he was hurried away. Having now gained considerable knowledge of their language, I learned that they were afraid that if we were permitted to hold converse, we should be the means of provoking the Supreme God, Anit, to do them some injury.

The bread fruit beginning to ripen, we were all employed in gathering it; and I will endeavor to give the reader an idea of the process of preserving it. After the fruit was gathered, the outside rind was scraped off, and the seeds taken out; which are in size and appearance like a chestnut. The fruit is then put into a net, the meshes of which are quite small, taken into the salt water, and then beaten with a club to pumice. It is then put into baskets made of cocoanut leaves, and in about two days becomes like a rotten apple; after which the cores are taken out, and the remainder, after undergoing a process of kneading, is put into a hole in the ground, the bottom and sides of which are neatly inlaid with leaves, and left about two days; when it again undergoes the same process of kneading, and so on until it is perfectly dry. This occupied us a number of days; and when we were engaged in gathering another, and a larger kind, a small boy came running towards us, and exclaimed, "Uroit aro rayta mony la Wirrum," that is, the chiefs are going to kill William. Ludjuan seeing that I understood what the boy said, replied "Reab-reab!" it is false. From the pains taken by the natives to keep Hussey and myself apart, it was evident that they were in some measure afraid of us; but from what cause I had yet to learn. After passing a sleepless night, we again in the morning pursued our labors, but I was continually agitated by fearful apprehensions. About midnight I overheard some of the natives in the tent talking about me, and I was now convinced that some injury was contemplated. I then asked them what I was to be killed for. They seemed surprised when I told them I had been listening; yet they denied that I was to be killed, and one of them who had frequently manifested for me much friendship, came to my mat, and lay down with me, assuring me I should not be injured.

The harvest being ended, a feast was had, and the chiefs were presented with considerable quantities of this fruit, after it had been prepared and baked, which in taste resembled a sweet potato, sending presents of it in all directions about the island.

Having now but little work to do, I confined myself to the hut as much as possible, for I had been observed for some time in a very suspicious manner. In a few days I was informed that Hussey had been brought to the island, and it was immediately suggested to my anxious mind, that we were now to be sacrificed. Ludjuan went with me to see Hussey, but we were only allowed a few moments' conversation, when I was taken back to the hut, and communicated my fears to my old mistress, who sympathized with me, but said if the chiefs determined it, there was no hope for me. I was now made acquainted with the cause of their dislike, which was no less than a superstitious idea, that we were the cause of a malady, then raging to a considerable extent.

This disease consisted in the swelling of the hands and feet, and in many instances the faces of the youth swelled to such a degree, that they were blind for a number of days. Such a disease they had never before been afflicted with. I now had an opportunity of most solemnly protesting my total inability to injure them in this way, and as the disease had as yet caused no death, I had a hope of being spared. I learned that a majority of the chiefs in council, were for putting me to death, but one of them in particular, protested against it, fearing it might be a cause of some worse calamity. As the vote to carry into effect any great measure, must be unanimous, this chief was the means, by his dissenting, of saving my life.

The afflicted began to recover, and my fears.

were greatly lessened; but as these people are of a very unstable and changeful character, I could not entirely divest myself of apprehensions.

As soon as the harvest was completed, great preparations were made for the embarkation of the chiefs, who were going to make their annual visit to the different islands. They told me their king, whom they called Laboowoole, yet lived on an island at the northwest, and if he did not receive his yearly present of preserved bread fruit and pero, he would come with a great party to fight them. Twelve canoes were put in the water, each one carrying a part of the provisions, and manned by about two hundred persons.

After an absence of four or five days, during which time we exchanged civilities with numerous chiefs, we returned to Milly, and hauled up the canoes. I now learned that the principal chief, had said it would have been wrong to kill me; firmly believing that the disease with which they had been afflicted, had been sent by their God, as a punishment for having killed Payne and the others. The malady having now entirely disappeared, they considered that the crime was expiated.

About two days after my return, there was great excitement, in consequence of the appearance of a ship. Seeing the natives were very much displeased at the circumstance, I concealed as well as I could, the gladdening emotions which filled my breast; and, surrounded by about three hundred of them, went round a point of land, when I distinctly saw a ship standing for the land. The displeasure of the natives increased; they demanded to know where she came from, how many men she had in her, etc. I was compelled to tell them that she was not coming to get me, and even pretended to be afraid of her approach, which pleased them much, as they appeared determined I should never leave them. At dusk she was so near the land, that I saw them shorten sail, and fondly anticipated the hour of my deliverance as not far distant.

During the night, sleep was a stranger to me, and with the most anxious emotions did I anticipate the welcome reception on board, and above all, a happy and joyful landing on my native shore. In the morning, Ludjuan went with me to the beach, but, alas! no ship was in sight. She had vanished, and with her fled all my hopes of a speedy deliverance. The kind reader can perhaps form some idea of my disappointment.

The natives continued to be kind to me, and I was often complimented by them for my knowledge of their language; and the appearance of my person had very much improved, my hair and beard being long, and my skin turned nearly as black as their own. I was often importuned to have my ears bored and stretched, but never gave my consent, which much surprised them, it being a great mark of beauty. They begin at the age of four years; and perforate the lower part of the ear, with a sharp stick, and as the ear stretches, larger ones are inserted, until it will hang nearly to their shoulders. The larger the ear, the more beauty the person possesses.

About a fortnight after I saw the ship pass, Hussey came with his master, on a visit. His disappointment was great, and we could only cheer each other by hoping for the best, and wait patiently the pleasure of Heaven.

Hussey again left me, and we parted under less bodings of evil than before, for the kindness of the natives began to increase, and their suspicions to be allayed.

I will here acquaint the reader with some of the means that I was induced to make use of, to satisfy the cravings of appetite. As the island now was in a state of almost entire famine, my daily subsistence not amounting to more (upon an average) than the substance of one half a cocoanut each day. The chief I lived with, having several cocoanut trees that he was very choice of, and which bore plentifully, I would frequently (after the natives in the hut were all soundly asleep) take the opportunity and get out of the hut unperceived, and climb one of those trees (being very careful about making the least noise, or letting any of them drop to the ground, whereby I might be detected), and take the stem of one cocoanut in my mouth, and one in each hand, and in that manner make out to slide down

95

the tree, and would then with my prize, make the best of my way to a clump of bushes, at a considerable distance from the hut, where I would have a sumptuous repast; and if any remained, would secrete it, until by hunger, I was driven to the necessity of revisiting that place.

I made a practice of this for some time, until the chief began to miss his cocoanuts, and keep such watch, that I, for fear of being detected, was obliged to relinquish that mode of satisfying my appetite.

A short time after this, I ventured to take a cocoanut off the ground where the natives had recently buried a person; a deed which is strictly against the laws of their religious principles (if it can be said that they have any), and a deed which the natives never dare to do, for fear of displeasing the God, Anit, under a certain length of time after the person had been buried, and then, the spot is only to be approached by males.

Not twenty-four hours had elapsed after I took the cocoanut, before they missed it, and coming immediately to me, charged me with taking it, telling me that not a native on the island would have dared so much as to handle it, for fear of the bad spirit (Anit).

I then told them that I had taken it, but pleading ignorance in the case, and promising never to do anything of the like again, and making it appear to them that I was surprised at what they told me of the bad spirit, and also that I believed the same, they left me, after telling me that if I ever handled another of them, it would not only bring sickness and death upon myself, but would bring it upon the whole island.

The reader will naturally suppose that my mind was considerably relieved on their leaving me so soon, fearing that something serious might be the result.

After this I was very careful how I did anything I thought would in the least displease, or irritate them, and made myself content with the portion they saw fit to give me.

I frequently fired a musket to please them, by their request, and told them if they would let me have some powder, I would fire off the swivel, left by the Globe. They consented, and collected in great numbers, and after I had loaded the gun with a heavy charge, I told them they had better stand back. They said I must set her on fire, and tell them when she was going off, and they would run. I, however, touched her off, when they immediately fell on their faces in the greatest panic. When their fears had subsided, they set up howling and yelling with ecstacy.

They said, if they should have a battle, I must carry that gun with me, which would alone vanquish their enemies.

We were visited by eight or ten canoes, from a distant island, called Alloo. They came to exchange presents with our chiefs, and very soon a great quantity of pero, etc., was baked, and having been inspected by the chiefs, to see that it was in a proper state to be presented to their visitors, it was given them to eat.

As these people had never seen me before, I was much annoyed by them. During their stay, I was constantly surrounded; my skin felt of, and often made the sport of the more witty.

98

because my skin was not of so dark a hue as their own, and more especially, as my ears remained in the same form as when nature gave them to me. These visitors, to my great satisfaction, did not remain long with us.

Their mode of anchoring their canoes is singular. One of them takes the end of a line, and diving to the bottom, secures it to a rock; and in the same way do they dive down to cast it off. I have seen them do this in five fathoms of water.

CHAPTER VI.

It was not until the 23d of November, 1825, that the prospects of being relieved from my disagreeable situation began to brighten. Early in the morning of that day, I was awakened by a hooting and yelling of the natives, who said a vessel had anchored at the head of the island. They seemed alarmed, but I need not assure the reader, that my feelings were of a contrary nature. Their God was immediately consulted, as to the measures to pursue; but as I was not allowed to be present when he was invoked, I cannot say what was the form of this ceremony, except that cocoanut leaves were used. Their God, however, approved the plan, which was, that they should go to the vessel, or near her, to swim on board, a few at a time, until two hundred were on board, and then a signal

100

was to be given, when they were to throw the persons on board into the water, and kill them. Two large canoes, which would carry fifty men each, were put in readiness, but at first they refused to let me accompany them, fearing that I would inform of their having killed our men, and they would be punished. I assured them that the vessel, having but two masts, did not belong to my nation, and I was certain I could not speak their language.

They at length consented for me to go. We arrived within a few miles of the vessel at night, and early the following morning, we were joined by a number of canoes, which made in all two hundred men. It being squally in the forenoon, we remained where we were, but when it cleared up, the yells of the Indians announced the approach of the vessel. I had only time to see that it was really an armed schooner, when I was secreted with their women, about forty in number, in a hut near the shore, and the women had orders to watch me closely, that I did not get away.

The Globe Mutiny.

A boat at this time from the schooner, was seen approaching the shore. She landed at about a hundred yards distant from where I was confined; but it being near night, I soon found she was making the best of her way towards the schooner. Night came, and I was sent for by the principal chief, and questioned closely concerning the schooner. My fears and apprehensions were now excited to a degree beyond human expression, and the kind reader will pardon all attempts to express them.

The natives seeing the whites so bold, excited in them a fear which induced them to flee the island. Accordingly, about midnight, the canoes were launched, and I was carried to a remote part of the island, a distance of about forty miles, where I remained until my fortunate escape.

29th. Early in the morning, we discovered a boat under sail, standing directly for the place where we were; the natives were considerably agitated with fear, and engaged in planning some method by which to overcome the people in the boat, if they should come where we were; and, as

The Globe Mutiny.

I expected the natives would hide me, as they had heretofore done, I thought it best to offer my services to assist them. I said I would aid them in fighting the boat's crew, and that, as I could talk with them, I would go to them, in advance of the natives, deceive the crew, and prevail on them to come on shore and sit down, and for us to appear friendly till in possession of their arms, then rise upon the crew and kill them without difficulty or hazard. Some of the natives suspected that I should revolt to the other party, and turn the current of destruction upon them; but the Chief Luttnon said he liked my plan much, and would inquire of their God, and if he found that I should be true to them, my plan should be adopted. The inquiry resulted in favor of my plan, and they said I might go. The boat was now within one hundred rods of the shore, and Luttnon called me to him, oiled my head and body with cocoanut oil, and gave me my charge how to conduct. I pledged myself to obey his orders. My joy at this moment was great, as the boat anchored near where we were. I went to

the beach accompanied by about one hundred of
the smartest natives, whom I charged not to
manifest a hostile appearance. I hailed the boat
in English, and told the crew what the calcula-
tions of the natives were, and not to land unless
they were well armed. The officer of the boat
replied that he would be among them directly;
and in a few minutes they landed, 13 men and 2
officers, and when within a rod of us I ran to
Lieut. H. Paulding, who took me by the hand,
asked if I was one of the Globe's crew, and inquired my name, etc., etc. We then retreated
to the boat, facing the natives, who all kept their
seats, excepting the 'one I called father, who
came down among us, and took hold of me to
carry me back, but desisted on having a pistol
presented to his breast.

Lieut. Hiram Paulding, of the Navy, for such
was the name of this gentlemanly officer, informed me that the vessel was the U. S.
Schooner Dolphin, sent on purpose to rescue us,
and commanded by Lieut.-Com. John Percival.

After expressing my gratitude as well as I was

able, to Heaven, which had furnished the means of my deliverance, I acquainted Mr. Paulding, that the only survivor of the Globe, except myself, was Cyrus M. Hussey; who was held in bondage upon a neighboring island. After the boat's crew had taken some refreshment, we left the landing place, and soon arrived at the place where Hussey lived. The natives had concealed him, but after some threatening from us, restored him, and we were received on board the Dolphin and treated in the most kind and hospitable manner.

Our hair was now cut, and we were shaved. Our appearance must have been truly ludicrous, our hair having been growing twenty-two months, untouched by the razor or scissors.

Our joy and happiness on finding ourselves on board an American man-of-war, and seeing the "star spangled banner" once more floating in the air, we will not attempt to describe. Suffice it to say, that none can form a true estimate of our feelings, except it be those who have been suddenly and unexpectedly rescued from pain and peril, and threatening death. In the afternoon, the captain wished me to go on shore with him, as an interpreter. We accordingly went, and passed over to the village on the other side of the island, where we had an interview with a woman of distinction, the men having fled, being principally absent with the chiefs at Alloo. The captain informed her he wished to see the chiefs, and requested her to send for them that night, that he might visit them in the morning, and make them some presents. We then returned to the vessel; and the following day, December 1st, went on shore for the purpose of seeing the chiefs, but could not obtain an interview with them. The captain informed the natives that he must see the chiefs; and that he would wait another day; but if disappointed then, he should be compelled to use coercive means. They immediately sent another messenger after them, and we returned on board, accompanied by several of the natives, among whom was Ludjuan. The captain made him several presents, and informed

The Globe Mutiny.

him they were given as a compensation for saving my life. Shortly after, the natives went on shore.

The next morning, December 2d, the captain sent me on shore, to ascertain whether the chiefs had returned; and I was informed by the natives that they had, and were then at a house half a mile distant. This intelligence having been communicated to the captain, he went on shore, and took myself and Hussey for interpreters; but we found, on our arrival, that the natives had been practising a piece of deception—the chiefs not having returned. Very much displeased at this perfidious treatment, the captain made a demand of the chiefs before sunset; threatening, if it were not complied with, to go on shore with fifty men, well armed, and destroy every person he could find. This threat threw the natives into consternation and immediately another messenger was dispatched for the chiefs. The natives were so alarmed, that they soon sent off three or four more messengers; and we returned on board, to dine. After dinner, I went on shore with Mr. Paulding, the first Lieutenant, and some of the under officers, for the purpose of shooting birds. After rambling round the island for some time, we discovered a number of natives quickly approaching us from the lower part of the island; and supposing the chiefs were with them, we sat down to await their arrival; but before they came to us, a signal was set on board the schooner for us to return; which was immediately obeyed, without waiting for an interview with the natives. Early on the next morning, I was sent ashore to ascertain whether the chiefs had arrived, and so found that they had; they were in a hut, waiting to receive a visit from the captain, who, I informed them, would come on shore after breakfast, to have a talk with them, and also to bestow some presents. Accordingly, the captain with myself and Hussey, repaired to the hut, where we found them sitting, and ready to commune with us.

The captain told them he had been sent out by the Head Chief of his country, to look for the men that had been left there by the ship Globe— that he had been informed they murdered all but

two—that, as it was their first offense of the
kind, their ignorance would plead an excuse—
but if they should ever kill or injure another white
man, who was from any vessel or wreck, or who
might be left among them, our country would
send a naval force, and exterminate every soul on
the island; and also destroy their fruit trees,
provisions, etc., and that if they would always
treat white men kindly, they would never receive
any injury from them, but would have their kindness and hospitality reciprocated. He also ad-
verted to the practice of stealing, lying, and other
immoralities; stating to the natives that these
crimes are abhorred and punished in our country;
and that murder is punished by death. He then
sent me to the boat, lying at the beach, to bring
three tomahawks, one axe, a bag of beads, and a
number of cotton handkerchiefs, which were presented to the chiefs. He also gave them two
hogs, and a couple of cats, with injunctions not
to destroy them; that they might multiply. The
captain caused potatoes, corn, pumpkins, and
many valuable seeds to be planted, and gave the

natives instructions how to raise and preserve them. He then explained to them that these acts of kindness and generosity were extended because they saved us alive, and had taken care of us while among them. This conversation with the natives being ended, we went on board, dined, and the captain and Hussey went again on shore. The first Lieutenant made preparations for cruising in the launch, around the island, to make topographical surveys, who took me with him, as interpreter, and about four o'clock, we commenced a cruise with a design to sail up an inlet or inland sea; but the wind blowing fresh, and having a head sea, at twelve o'clock, we anchored for the night.

December 4th. At sunrise we found ourselves not more than a mile from the place where we crossed over the evening before; and immediately getting under way, and rowing to the westward, we soon came to the place, where the Globe's station had been; anchored, and went on shore, for the purpose of disinterring the bones of Comstock, who had been buried there, and to obtain the cutlass which was buried with him; but before we had accomplished the undertaking, the schooner got under way, and soon anchored abreast of us, at the same place where the Globe's provisions were landed. The captain and Hussey came on shore to view the place; but as I caught cold the preceding night, by lying exposed in our launch, I was excused from serving further with Mr. Paulding, in making surveys; and Hussey supplied my place. Soon after, I went on board with the captain, carrying with me the skull of the person we had dug up, and the cutlass, intending to convey them to America.

After dinner, the captain made a trip in the gig, to Allōo, taking me for his interpreter, where we arrived in half an hour, and soon travelled up to the village. The natives received us with marks of gladness, and in a short time, the house at which we stopped was surrounded by them, who came undoubtedly for the purpose of gratifying their curiosity, by gazing at us. We remained at the village about two hours, during which time we had considerable talk with two of the chief women, and made some small presents to the people, such as beads, etc. They did not treat us as they usually do visitors, with fruit, etc., there being at that time, what we call a famine, which in their language, is Ingathah.

After having taken leave of the natives, and walked about half the distance to the shore, we stopped to rest ourselves under a fine, cool shade tree. While in conversation on the manners and customs of the natives, an old man and woman approached us, who had acted towards me, during my residence among them, as father and mother. I immediately made them and their kindness to me, known to the captain, who, in consideration of their humane treatment, rewarded them with a few beads and a handkerchief, for which they appeared thankful and grateful—telling them at the same time, the presents were to recompense their hospitality to me, and enjoining on them at all times to be friendly to the whites, and a reward would certainly await them. It being near the close of the day, we left Alloo, and having a fair wind, reached the schooner before dark.

The Globe Mutiny.

The next morning, December 5th, being very
pleasant, all hands were employed in procuring
wood for the schooner—some in cutting it down,
and others in boating it off. Our carpenter had
been engaged for a few days, at Milly; to in-
struct and assist the natives in repairing a canoe.
The distance was four or five miles, and the captain wanting the carpenter, set sail for Milly, in
his gig, and soon arrived there; where he learned
that the carpenter had repaired the canoe, to the
great satisfaction of the natives, who expressed
a strong desire that he might be permitted to remain among them on the island; but the captain
informed them he could not spare him. When
the natives saw the carpenter packing up his tools,
they expressed to me an expectation that the tools
would be left with them as a present. We left
the natives, and reached the schooner a little before sunset; the captain feeling anxious for the
fate of the launch, as nothing yet, had been heard
of the fortune which had attended her, or the men
in her.

December 6th. Having procured a sufficient

supply of wood, though our supply of provisions was hardly sufficient for the voyage, and the launch having returned, at about 10 A.M., we weighed anchor, and proceeded to the place called Milly, where we anchored for the purpose of planting some seeds, and taking a last farewell of the chiefs and their people. The captain went immediately on shore, taking Hussey for his interpreter. He was gone till nearly night, when he returned, bringing with him Luttnon and several other natives. The captain gave orders to beat to quarters, to exhibit the men to the natives, and explain to them the manner of our fighting. These untutored children of nature seemed highly gratified with the maneuvers; but were most delighted with the music, probably the first of the kind they had ever heard. We informed them we always have such music when we are fighting an enemy. The natives were then landed, and we immediately made sail for the head of the island, intending to cruise around the other shores of it, for the purpose of making surveys, and constructing a map of it. We stood eastward till nearly morning, then altered our course, and headed towards the island.

During the following day, December 7th, having favorable winds and weather, we made a regular survey of the whole length of the group, before sunset. The captain now steered N. W. to endeavor to discover other islands which the natives had often described to me, during my abode with them. They said they had frequently visited ten or twelve different islands in their canoes, and that the people who inhabited them all speak the same language, which is the same as their own, and that the islands lie about one day's sail from each other.

December 8th. The weather pleasant and fair; about 9 A.M., we saw land ahead, and passed it on the windward side; then varied our course and sailed to the leeward of the island; but night coming on, we were obliged to defer landing till morning. The captain then attempted to reach the shore in the gig; but was not able to land, on account of the surf. After he returned on board, we made sail, cruising farther to the leeward, in hopes of finding a place to anchor, but in this we were disappointed, not being able to find bottom thirty yards from the rocks. However, at high water, the captain, at imminent hazard in passing the surf, succeeded in landing. He had previously given orders to Hussey and me, not to let the natives know that we could converse with, or understand them; but to be attentive to everything that might pass among them, to ascertain whether their intentions and dispositions were hostile or friendly. After landing, the captain and Hussey visited the house where the head chief or king of all those islands lived, of whom I had formerly heard so much, while I was on the Mulgraves. They continued with him about two hours, were treated well, and discovered nothing unfriendly in the natives. The captain told Hussey he might make them acquainted with his knowledge of their language, by conversing with them. The king, on hearing Hussey speaking in the language of the natives, appeared at first so frightened and agitated, that he could scarcely reply; but by degrees became composed, and inquired of Hussey where he learned their language, and why he had not spoken to them immediately on coming ashore. Hussey then informed him he was one of the two persons that had been on the Mulgraves (in their language, Milly), and that the other person (myself), was on board the schooner—that the schooner had been there after us; that we left the Mulgraves, the day before, and had then visited that island for the purpose of examining it, etc., etc. The king had long before heard of our being at the Mulgraves, and told Hussey he had been repairing his canoe, in order to go to those islands, with a view to induce us to live with him, who, had that been the case, would undoubtedly have used us well. The king was about seventy years of age, and had a daughter on the island where we had resided, wife to Luttnon. He inquired if his daughter was alive and well, with tears in his eyes, and trembling form, for it was a long time since he had received any intelligence of her; and hearing of her welfare so unexpectedly, quite overcame the good old father's feelings. And here the reader will observe, that the pure and unaffected emotions produced by parental affection are similar among all the human species, whether civilized or savage. The natives of the island we were then visiting, may be ranked with those that have made the fewest approaches towards the refined improvements of enlightened nations, yet the ground work of humanity was discovered to be the same; and the solicitude of a fond father for a beloved child, was manifested in a manner which would not disgrace those who move in the most elevated circles of civilized life. The old king expressed his regret that he had not visited the Mulgraves during our stay there, was very sorry we were about to return to America, and used all the force of native eloquence, to persuade us to continue with him. He inquired if we had got the whale boat he had heard of our having at the Mulgraves. Hussey informed him it was on board the schooner, and the swivel likewise. The captain then informed the king that he wanted cocoanuts and bup, which were obtained; and in return, the captain gave the natives some beads and handkerchiefs. The captain then went on board the schooner, made sail, standing a N. W. course, in pursuit of another island.

December 9th. About 10 o'clock in the forenoon, we discovered land ahead and off our lee bow. About 2 P.M., we arrived near the land, hove the schooner to, and sent two boats ashore, to get provisions. At sunset the boats returned, loaded with cocoanuts and bup. We hoisted up our boats, and with a strong breeze, it being the inclement season of the year, prosecuted our voyage to the Sandwich Islands, and had much boisterous weather during the passage.

On the 8th of January, 1826, we expected to make one of the Sandwich Islands, called Bird's Island, but night came on before we discovered it. But early on the following morning, we saw land about four leagues to the leeward, and bore to the island for the purpose of sending a boat ashore, to kill seals. We arrived near the landing place, hove to, and the captain with six men

went ashore in the whale boat. We now stood
off from the shore about an hour, then tacked and
stood to, for the boat to come off. The wind
had increased to almost a gale, and continuing
to blow harder, when we were within a quarter
of a mile off the island, not discovering anything
of the boat, we veered off again, and continued
tacking till night came on, but saw nothing of
the boat or her crew. About 9 or 10 o'clock,
the wind abated, and we found ourselves two
leagues to the leeward of the island, where we
lay to all night under easy sail, anxiously waiting
for the approach of morning, in hopes then to
learn the fate of the captain and men who had
gone on shore. At length the horizon was
lighted by the dawn of day, which was succeeded
by the opening of a very pleasant morning. We
immediately made all sail for the island; but
having a head wind, we did not arrive at the
landing till near the middle of the day. A boat
was sent on shore to learn what had befallen the
crew of the whale boat, and shortly returned with
all the men except the captain, and one man that

could not swim. We ascertained, that in attempting to come off through the surf, they were swamped and lost their boat. We, a second time, sent the boat ashore, with means to get the captain and other man, who were soon brought on board. We now made sail and steered our course for Woahoo, one of the Sandwich Islands, and nothing very material occurring on our passage, we anchored in the harbor of that island on the 14th. On the 16th, procured a supply of fresh provisions. On the 19th, Hussey and I went on shore for the purpose of rambling round the island; but nothing occurred worthy of notice.

Our foremast being found rotten a few feet below the top, it was deemed necessary to take it out for repairs, which required the daily employment of the carpenter and others for some time. On the 27th, the captain received a letter, giving intelligence that the ship London had been driven ashore at an island not far distant from Woahoo. As the Dolphin's foremast was out, the captain was under the necessity of pressing the brig Convoy, of Boston; and putting on board of her, about ninety of his own men, taking with him, two of his lieutenants, and some under officers, he sailed to the assistance of the ship London.

February 3d, the brig Convoy returned laden with a part of the cargo of the London, and the specie which was in her at the time of her going ashore, under the command of our second lieutenant, leaving the remainder of her cargo in another vessel, under the command of Captain Percival.

February 5th. The captain returned with the residue of the London's cargo, and the officers and crew of that ship. After the cargo of the London had been secured, we were employed in finishing the repairs on our foremast, which were completed on the 21st; then we commenced rigging.

February 26th. On the morning of this day, permission was granted to a number of our crew, to go on shore. In the afternoon, Hussey and I went ashore and took a walk. About 4 or 5 o'clock,

The Globe Mutiny.

I observed a great collection of natives, and on inquiring the reason, learned that several of the Dolphin's crew, joined by some from other ships lying in port, had made an assault upon Mr. Bingham, the missionary, in consequence of ill will towards that gentleman, strongly felt by some of the sailors; but for what particular reason, I did not distinctly ascertain. They carried their revenge so far, that they not only inflicted blows upon Mr. Bingham, but attacked the house of a chief. The natives, some with cutlasses, and others with guns, repelled the unjustifiable attack; and during the affray, several of our men were slightly injured, and one badly wounded, whose life was despaired of for some time. The offenders were arrested, sent on board, and put in irons.

On the next day, the 27th, Mr. Bingham came on board with the captain and witnesses against the men engaged the preceding day, in the assault on shore. After a fair examination of evidence in the case, the aggressors were properly punished, and ordered to their duty. The

123

whale ships now began to arrive for the purpose of recruiting, and for some particular reasons, several of the captains of those ships requested Captain Percival to remain at the island as a protection to them, till they could obtain the necessary supplies, and resume their cruises. From the present date, nothing of importance occurred that would be interesting to readers, till April 3d, when great preparations were made on board the Dolphin, to give a splendid entertainment to the young king. The gig and second cutter were employed in the morning, to borrow signals from the different ships in the harbor, in order to dress out the schooner in a fanciful style. About 11 o'clock, the gig and second cutter were sent ashore for the king and several chiefs and natives of distinction, who were soon conveyed on board. The yards were manned, and a general salute fired. After partaking of as good a dinner as our resources and the means within our reach would afford, the king and his attendants were disembarked under the honor of another salute. During the remainder of this month, the events which transpired, were principally of an ordinary cast, and not thought worthy of record.

May 3d. This day we were employed in bending sails; and from this date to the 11th, the necessary preparations were made to commence our homeward voyage. This day, (11th), the pilot came on board, and for the last time we weighed our anchors in the harbor of Woahoo. While retiring from the shore we were saluted with twenty-one guns from the fort. We hove about, returned the salute, and then resumed our destined course, and bid a last adieu to Woahoo, after a tedious and protracted stay of about four months.

From the time of our departure, on the 11th of May, from Woahoo, nothing of importance transpired till the 12th of June. On the morning of this day we discovered the Island of Toobowy; and at 9 o'clock, saw a sail, which proved to be a whale ship. At half-past two, came to anchor at a convenient place near the island, and sent a boat ashore, which returned at

night with two natives, who gave us a description of the harbor, and directions how to enter
it; and as our main mast was injured, we entered it to make the necessary repairs. On the
13th, we beat up the harbor; at 3 o'clock,
anchored, where we continued repairing our
mast, and procuring wood and water, till the
22d; when we weighed anchor and made sail
for Valparaiso, favored with fine weather and
good winds. July 18th, we made the Island of
Massafuero, and passed it about midnight. On
the 19th, in the forenoon, made the Island of
Juan Fernandez; and at 11 P.M., on the following day discovered the land at the south of Valparaiso. On the 22d, beat up the harbor, and at 2
o'clock on the morning of the 23d, came to
anchor. At Valparaiso, we learned that the
frigate United States was at Callao; and after
getting a supply of provisions we sailed for
Callao on the 9th of August, and arrived on the
24th. Here we found the United States lying
under the Island of Lorenzo, with several English ships of war.

The Globe Mutiny.

On the 26th, the Dolphin in company with the United States, passed over to Callao; and September 1st, I and the crew of the Dolphin were transferred to the United States.

September 10th. All the men that had been transferred from the Dolphin to the United States had liberty to go to Lima; at 12 o'clock we went on shore, and at 4 P.M., entered the gates of the city. I employed my time while on shore, in roving about the city, and viewing the various objects it presents; and on the 13th, returned on board the United States. We were detained here till the 16th of December, when we sailed for Valparaiso, and having a pleasant passage, arrived on the 6th of January, where we were happy to find, for our relief, the Brandywine. From the 8th to the 24th, all hands were engaged in preparing the ship for her homeward voyage; when at 9 o'clock we weighed our larboard anchor, and at 1 P.M., were under sail, passing out of the harbor, when the Cambridge (an English 74), then lying in the harbor, gave us three cheers, which we returned with three times three; she then saluted us with thirteen guns, which we returned with the same number, and then proceeded to sea.

Being favored with fine weather and good winds, we had a prosperous voyage to Cape Horn, and arrived off the pitch on the 7th of February, and passed around with a pleasant breeze. In prosecuting our voyage home, off the mouth of the river Rio de la Plata, and along the coast of Brazil we had rough weather and thick fogs. On the 6th, we made the land and harbor of St. Salvador; and about 9 o'clock came to anchor. On the 7th, we fired a salute for the fort, which was returned.

We were now employed in watering our ship, and making other preparations for continuing our voyage homeward; and on the 15th, got under way, with a fine breeze.

April 1st. At 10 o'clock, made the Island of Barbadoes, and at 1 P.M., came to anchor, where we lay till 5 P.M., on the 3d, when we got under way, and sailed down to the Island of St. Thomas, where we sent a boat ashore, and after transacting the business for which we stopped, made sail on the 9th, for the port of New York. On the 21st, made the highlands of Neversink; at 2 P.M., took a pilot on board, but owing to fogs and calms, did not arrive at the port of destination till 1 P.M., next day, when we anchored opposite the West Battery, with a thankful heart that I was once more within the United States.

CHAPTER VII.

I WILL now proceed to give the reader some account of the islands I visited, and of the manners and customs of the natives, and shall endeavor to be as candid and correct as possible.

The Mulgrave Islands are situated between 5 and 6° north latitude, and between 170 and 174° east longitude. They are about fifty miles in length, and lie in the form of a semicircle, forming a kind of inland sea or lake; the distance across it being about twenty miles. The land is narrow, and the widest place is probably not more than half a mile. On the north side of the group are several inlets or passages, of sufficient depth to admit the free navigation of the largest ships; and if explored, excellent harbors would in all probability be found. In the inland sea are numerous beds of coral, which appear to be constantly forming and increasing.

The Globe Mutiny.

These corals beds are seen at low water, but are all overflowed at high tide. The whole group is entirely destitute of mountains, and even hills, the highest land not being more than six feet above the level of the sea at high water. By the accounts given me from the natives, it appears that some parts have been overflowed by the sea. Their being so low, makes the navigation near them very dangerous in the night, both because they would not be easily seen, and because the water is very deep, quite to the shores; and a place for anchoring can scarcely be found on the outside of the island.

The air of these islands is pure, and the climate hot; but the heat is rendered less oppressive by the trade winds, which blow constantly, and keep the atmosphere healthful and salubrious for so low a latitude.

The soil, in general, is productive of little besides trees and shrubs, and most of it is covered with rough coral stones.

The productions are bread fruit in its proper season, and cocoanuts, which they have throughout the year; and a kind of fruit different from any that grows in America, which the natives call bup—all growing spontaneously. Of the leaves of the trees the women manufacture very elegant mats, which they wear as blankets and clothing; of the bark of a vine they make the men's clothing; and of the husks of the cocoa they make ropes and rigging for their canoes, and for almost every other purpose. The waters around the islands abound with fish, and the natives are very expert in catching them.

There are no animals on the islands, excepting rats; and by these little quadrupeds, they were literally overrun.

The number of all the inhabitants, men, women, and children, is probably between five and six hundred.

The following may be given as prominent characteristics of the natives. They are, in general, well made and handsome—very indolent and superstitious. They are morose, treacherous, ferociously passionate, and unfriendly to all other natives. When they are not fishing or otherwise employed, they are generally travelling about, and visiting each other. They have no salutations when they meet, but sit down without exchanging a word of civility for some minutes; but after a silent pause, the head of the family, if there is anything in the house to eat, presents it to his guests, who, when they have eaten sufficiently, if there are any fragments left, are very careful to secure them and carry them off when they return home; and the host would regard it as an imposition, if his visitors were to neglect this important trait of politeness and fashionable item in etiquette. They accustom themselves to frequent bathing; and commence with the children on the day of their birth, and continue the practice twice a day, regularly, till they are two years old. They do this to invigorate the system, and render the skin of their children thick and tough by exposure. Their living consists simply of bread fruit, cocoanuts, and bup; but cocoanuts are all they can depend on, the year round—the other two articles being common only a part of the year.

The Globe Mutiny.

Their diversions consist in singing, dancing, and beating time with their hands, in a manner similar to the amusements of the natives at the Sandwich Islands, in which they appear to take great delight.

They wear their hair long, and tie it up in a kind of bow on the top of the head, and this is all the covering they have for their heads. The men have long beards. One part of their dress makes a singular and ludicrous appearance, which resembles two horse tails suspended from the waist, one before and the other behind. The women's dress consists of two mats, about the size of a small pocket-handkerchief, which they tie around them like an apron.

I never saw any form of marriage among them, but when a couple are desirous of being united, their parents have a talk together on the subject, and if the parties all agree to the union, the couple commence living together as man and wife; and I never knew of an instance of separation between them after they had any family. In a few instances polygamy prevailed.

The Globe Mutiny.

The following will give a pretty correct idea of their funeral rites and solemnities:

When a person dies, the inhabitants of the village assemble together, and commence drumming and singing, halloing and yelling; and continue their boisterous lamentations for about forty-eight hours, day and night, relieving each other as they require. This they do because they imagine it is diverting to the person deceased. They bury the body at a particular place, back of their houses; and use mats for a coffin. After the ceremony of interment is performed, they plant two cocoanut trees, one at the head and the other at the feet of the buried person. But if the trees ever bear fruit, the women are prohibited from eating thereof, for fear of displeasing the bad spirit, Anit. And here it may not be inappropriate to remind the reader, that Eve ate of the forbidden fruit, notwithstanding she knew it would displease the Good Spirit.

In their personal appearance, the natives are about the middle size, with broad faces, flat noses, black hair and eyes, and large mouths.

135

The Globe Mutiny.

In relation to literature, they are as ignorant as it is possible for people to be, having not the most distant idea of letters.

Concerning the religion of the untaught natives of the Mulgraves, the following remarks will give all the knowledge I am in possession of:

They believe there is an invisible spirit that rules and governs all events, and that he is the cause of all their sickness and distress; consequently they consider him to be a very bad being. But they have no belief in a good spirit, nor have they any modes of worship. It is a prevalent opinion among them, when they are sick, that the bad spirit rests upon them; and they believe that particular maneuvers and a form of words, performed round and said over the sick, will induce Anit, the bad spirit, to cease from afflicting, and leave the unfortunate sufferers. With regard to a future state of existence, they believe that the shadow, or what survives the body, is, after death, entirely happy; that it roves about at pleasure, and takes much delight in beholding everything that is

136

transacted in this world ; and as they consider the world as an extensive plain, they suppose the disembodied spirits travel quite to the edge of the skies, where they think white people live, and then back again to their native isles; and at times they fancy they can hear the spirits of departed friends whistling round their houses, and noticing all the transactions of the living. Singular as some of these notions and opinions may appear, there is much to be met with in Christendom equally at variance with reason; and I have heard from the pulpit, in New England, the following langnuage: "I have no doubt in my own mind that the blessed in Heaven look down on all the friends and scenes they left behind, and are fully sensible of all things that take place on earth !"

CHAPTER VIII.

This chapter and the concluding remarks of the narrative, will be collated from a journal kept by Cyrus M. Hussey; and if there appear occasionally some incidents similar to those recorded in the preceding account, it is believed the value and interest of this history will not be diminished by them. Hussey commences thus:

About the last of April, Lay and I were separated, destined to different islands, not knowing whether we should ever see each other again. At night we arrived at an island, and hauled up our canoe. We found but few natives; but among the number was the mother of the chief with whom I lived. She was very inquisitive respecting me, and talked so incessantly through the night that I could not sleep. The next morning we were employed in gathering bread fruit, for the purpose of curing it for

138

the winter. This employment continued about three months, during which time I was very uneasy about my situation. At intervals of leisure, when the old chief had no particular engagements to engross his attention, he would launch his canoe and go and search for fish; but my shoes having been taken from me, whenever I was employed round the rough shores of the island, my feet were so wounded that I could hardly walk. The natives now commenced the destruction of my clothing, and not being able to converse with them, I found it very difficult to preserve my apparel. They often requested me to divest myself of my clothing, and dress as they did, or rather, not dress at all. I made signs that the sun would burn me, if I should expose myself to its scorching rays. When they found that persuasion would not induce me to divest myself of clothing, they began to destroy my clothes, by tearing them in pieces. It was some time before I could understand their language, so as to inform them that the sun would burn my back; and being robbed of my clothes,

139

the powerful influence of the sun soon scorched me to such a degree, that I could scarcely lie down or take any rest.

About the latter part of July, William Lay and others came to the island in a canoe, to see me, being the first interview we had enjoyed since our separation, which was about three months previous. Lay informed me that the natives had taken his Bible from him and torn it up, and threatened his life. He informed me that it seemed to him as though he was robbed of that comfort which none in a Christian land are deprived of. We were soon parted; he in a canoe was taken to an island by the natives called Dilabu, and I went to my employment, repairing a canoe which was on the stocks. After I had finished the canoe, the natives prepared a quantity of bread fruit and fish for the chiefs; and on the following morning we set sail for an island called Milly, one of the largest in the group, at which resides the principal chief. We arrived just at night and were cordially received by the natives, who had assembled on the beach in great numbers, for the purpose of getting some fish which the old chief had brought with him. He then hauled his canoe on shore; and I again had the pleasure of seeing my fellow-sufferer, William Lay, after a month's separation. Since our first meeting we were not allowed to converse much together.

The old chief tarried at this island but a short time, and Lay and myself were once more separated. The old chief, his family, and myself, returned to the island which we had left two or three days before, called, in the language of the natives, Tabarawort; and he and his family commenced gathering bread fruit. As the old man with whom I lived had charge of several small islands, we found it difficult to gather the fruit as fast as it ripened; so that a considerable part fell to the ground and perished. In the meantime, while we were employed in gathering in the fruits of the earth, news came to the island, to inform the chief with whom I lived, that it was the intention of the highest chiefs to destroy us both (that is, myself and Lay), because a

141

severe sickness prevailed among them, and they being superstitious, supposed we were the occasion of it. I informed them that we could not have been the cause of the sickness, as no such sickness prevailed in our country; and that I never before had seen a similar disease. But still they talked very hard about us, and the highest chief sent to the chief I lived with, to have me brought to the Island of Milly, where Lay lived, in order that we might be killed together. Preparations having been made, the old chief, whom I called father, with his family and myself, set sail the next morning for Milly, where we arrived about sunset. He immediately went to see the chief of Milly, to inquire the circumstances relating to the necessity of taking our lives, leaving me and the rest of the family in the canoe. I shortly perceived William Lay and his master coming towards the canoe, which produced sensations hard to be described. Affectionate and sympathizing reader, what must have been our feelings and conversation at that moment, when nothing seemingly was presented to our view, but death? We were allowed an interview of only a few minutes, when we were again separated.

My master soon returned to the canoe, and entered into a very earnest conversation with his family, which, at the time, I did not fully understand; but found afterwards he was relating to his family his interview with the natives on the subject of taking our lives; and that if they killed me, they would first have to kill him, (my master), which they were unwilling to do.

The next morning I asked leave of my master to visit Lay, which he readily gave. I set out for the hut in company with my master's son; but on approaching it, Lay called out to me, to inform me not to come—that the natives did not like to have us together. On my turning to go back, Lay's master called to me to come. I went and sat down, and entered into conversation with Lay, to ascertain what the intentions of the natives were towards us. He told me it was the design of the high chief to kill us. I observed to him that we were in the hands of the natives; still there was a higher and more powerful Hand that could protect us, if it were the Divine pleasure so to do. I then bade him farewell, and returned to the canoe, never expecting to see each other again till we should meet on the tranquil ocean of eternity.

My master being now ready to return to his island, the canoe was launched, and we set sail, and arrived the same night, having been absent two days. The natives expressed much joy on seeing me return, and asked many questions of the chief of Milly; but I was unable to speak their language intelligibly, I could give them but little information. We then went on with our work as usual, which was fishing, etc., etc.

After having been at this island some time, my master's wife manifested an inclination to go and visit her friends, who lived at an island called in their language Luguonewort. After a successful excursion in fishing, we cooked a part, and took some bread fruit, and embarked, agreeably to the wishes of my master's wife, and arrived at Luguonewort in two days. The natives of the island gave us a cordial reception. We hauled up our canoe and remained some time among them. After our agreeable visit was ended, we returned to the other island, found the natives well, and that good care had been taken by the chief's mother, and old woman to whom the superintendence of things had been left.

About six months after the massacre of my shipmates, the brother of the native in whose possession I was, came to the island, and informed us that a ship had been seen to pass a day or two before, and that it caused great disturbance among the chiefs—that they thought it was the ship that left the islands (the Globe), and that she was in search of us. My old master immediately prepared his canoe to visit the chiefs, and he wanted also to inquire of me what I thought respecting the ship. We loaded our canoe and made sail for Milly, where the chiefs were. We arrived at night, and found a great number of natives collected on the beach, to see if we had any fish. We hauled up our canoe for the night, and the natives began to question me about the ship. I told them I did not know, concluding it would be good policy to say but little on the subject. The natives crowded round me in great numbers; and I did not see Lay till he came to me. I inquired of him what he had seen, and he informed me that there had been a ship in sight about a half an hour before sunset, and that she was near enough for him to see them take in their fore and mizzen-topgallant sails, but could give no definite account of her, as she was soon out of sight. We were not allowed to be together long; and I went to rest as usual, but could not sleep.——"Hope springs eternal in the human breast"——and hope that the ship which had been seen had come to deliver us from savages and transport us to our native country and dear friends, had an influence on my feelings more powerful than sleep, and imagination was busy through the night in picturing scenes of future happiness.

But the prospect of our being released from

146

our unpleasant situation was not very flattering. Early next morning I asked and obtained permission from my master, to pay a visit to Lay, before passing round to the opposite side of the island. Accompanied by master's son and several others, I went to the hut where Lay lived, and we had the pleasure of another interview; but it was of short duration, for we were not allowed to be together more than a quarter of an hour. I returned to my master's canoe, and there continued till the middle of the day; we then launched and set sail for Tabanawort, where we arrived the fore part of the night. Early the next morning, we prepared for a fishing cruise, had pretty good success and returned just before night, made a fire, cooked some fish, and ate a delicious supper.

Our canoe being leaky and very much out of repair, my master and I commenced taking her to pieces, for the purpose of re-building her; and we were occasionly employed upon her nearly two months, when we launched her, and commencing fishing business, had alternately good and bad success. One day we had the good fortune to enclose, in a kind of weir made for the purpose, a large quantity of fishes, and with a scoop-net we caught a plentiful supply. After cooking them, we set out with a quantity to dispose of to the chiefs of Milly, where we arrived before night, on the same day of sailing. Very soon after our arrival I saw Lay and his master approaching the canoe, and we once more had a short but pleasant interview. I inquired of Lay how he fared, as to food, etc. His reply was "Better than I expected," and that the natives were kind to him, always giving him his part. I informed him I had a basket of fish reserved for him as a present, which he requested me to keep till dark, that he might be enabled to carry them home without having them all begged by the natives. He came at night for the fish, and I retired, agreeably to my master's wishes to sleep in the canoe, to prevent the natives from stealing the remainder of the fish that were on board. The next morning my master was highly pleased to find that nothing was missing; and he gave me liberty to go and see Lay. I went to the hut and found him with his master. They gave me a cordial welcome, and presented me with some cocoanuts in return for the fish. Lay's master inquired of me very particularly respecting my master, and the quantity of fish we caught. I then returned to the canoe carrying the cocoanuts, to deposit in the hold. My master asked me where I got them; I told him Lay's master gave them to me. If this minute detail should appear unimportant to the reader, he may draw a moral from it; for it evinces that my master was like other masters, desirous of knowing if his servant came honestly in possession of the cocoanuts. He then ordered me and his son to launch the canoe, which we did, got under sail for the island we left the day before, and arrived back at night. We learned that during our absence the natives had caught a considerable quantity of fish; and in a few days we caught a large quantity more; loaded our canoe, and embarked for one of the head islands to pay a visit, where we stopped some time. On our return, we commenced catching a kind of fish called by the natives, kierick. They are about the size of a small codfish; and the manner of taking them is very curious—they make a line of the husk of cocoanuts, about the size of a cod line; they then in the canoe pass round the fish to the windward of the flat, then lie to till a considerable quantity of them get on the flat, then square away by the wind and run down and go round the flat with this line, and thus catch them, men, women and children being employed. I have known them to catch one hundred at a draught. The fish are afraid of the line, and when enclosed, taken by a scoopnet. After taking a sufficient quantity, they go on shore to prepare for cooking them, which is done by digging a large hole in the earth, filling it with wood, covered with stones. The wood is then consumed, which heats the stones—the fish are wrapped in leaves to prevent them from falling to pieces, then covered with green leaves, and cooked by the heat of the stones. About an hour is required to cook them sufficient for eating. Their manner of curing fish, is to split them, and dry them in the sun, without using salt. Thus cured, they will keep some time. While we were employed in fishing, Lay came to the island, in company with a native, to visit me; but did not stay long, for the chief sent for him, fearing, as I afterwards found out, that they should lose us. From some hints that had been dropped, a report had got in circulation that my master and Ludjuan (Lay's master), intended to leave their islands, and embark for an island to the northwest, where the king lived, and carry us with them as a great curiosity. Lay was carried back to the chiefs—the head one sent a command to my master and Lay's, to come and see him—they made preparations and set sail for Milly; where they were closely questioned respecting their going to the other island, etc., etc. They denied that they had even intimated any such design; which was false, for I had frequently heard them talking on the subject myself; but kept silent, as it appeared to be a great crime for any to desert their island; and I feared the consequences of making it known. They then parted in peace and friendship, and I and my master returned to our habitation.

We then went to an island to catch fish, and a disagreement taking place between two of the natives, about some trifling affair, the particulars of which I did not learn, one of them took a spear belonging to the other, and after breaking it across his knee, with one half of it killed his antagonist, and left him. The parents of the man killed, being present, laid him out on some mats, and appeared to regret their loss very much. They kept up a continual drumming over the body of the deceased for two or three days; after which he received a decent burial on another island at some distance from the island where he was killed.

CHAPTER IX.

HAVING a successful fishing voyage, we loaded our canoe, and carried our cargo to the chiefs of Luguonewort. I had the satisfaction of an interview with Lay; but our provisions being soon exhausted, we were obliged to go again in search of fish. At this time there was a severe drought, and the bread fruit trees suffered extremely, many of them entirely died. The superstitious natives supposed the drought was sent upon them as a judgment, because myself and Lay were allowed to live. I informed them that we could neither make it rain nor prevent it; but some of them were so ignorant that they believed we could control the weather. But some of the chiefs thought the drought was visited upon them because they had killed our shipmates, and I was always ready to join them in that opinion. The drought continued about four months with such severity that most of the bread fruit trees on the small islands were so completely dried up that they never sprouted again. Many of the ignorant natives still insisted that their sickness and drought were occasioned by suffering us to live upon their islands; but this gross ignorance was counterbalanced by most of the chiefs, who believed differently, and to their more liberal opinion we were indebted for our lives.

About this time the islands were refreshed by plentiful showers of rain, and the natives assembled at Milly to sing for the bread fruit to come in abundance. They said their singing would please Anit, and that he would reward them with a very great crop.

A disturbance existed between the high chief and his brother Lougerene. The disagreement lasted about nine months, during which time the two brothers did not see or speak to each other. Luttnon, the high chief, then sent a canoe to inform his brother Lougerene that he wished to

see him. An interview took place, and a treaty
of peace was ratified.

During our stay at Milly, I had frequent op-
portunities of seeing Lay, my fellow-sufferer;
but the only relief we could afford each other
was derived from a sympathy of feelings, and in
conversations relating to our homes and native
country, by blending our mutual wishes for a
safe return, etc., etc. The reader can hardly
conceive the unpleasantness of our situation at
this time—the famine was so great that the tender branches of the trees were cooked, and the
nutritious juice drank as food. My strength
was so reduced in consequence of being deprived
of my usual quantity of provisions that I was
unable to accompany my master on a fishing voyage. When my master returned, he found me
lying in the hut, and asked me what was the
matter. I informed him my indisposition proceeded from hungry; he cooked a fish and gave
me, which, though it afforded me some relief,
was not half enough to satisfy the cravings of
appetite.

The Globe Mutiny.

After I had recruited my strength, one day while engaged in fishing, a canoe came to the island, and as soon as the canoe was near enough for the natives in her to be heard, they commenced hallooing, and making dreadful noises, which is their practice when war is declared. They informed us that the high chief had killed several of the lower chiefs who belonged to the island called Alloo; that Lougerene had fled to Alloo, his own island; and that the high chief was determined to pursue and kill him. We were ordered to go immediately to his assistance; accordingly we set sail for the island Milly, where we found a great number of natives collected for war. Again I had the satisfaction of being with Lay; who informed me that they were going to fight the other party at Alloo; and that the high chief had told him that he and I must prepare two muskets, and go and fight with them. Luttnon sent for me and Lay, and informed us he was about to have a battle, and that we must prepare to take part in it. We asked him if he had any powder—he said he had a plenty, and showed us a small box, which contained a little powder and mustard seed mixed together, which, if it had been good powder, would not have made more than five or six charges. We told him it was good for nothing; but he said we must do the best we could with it. As we were afraid to offend him, we went to work with the powder, and dried it in the sun and prepared our muskets for battle. The next morning we launched fifteen or sixteen canoes, and set sail for Alloo; where we arrived and landed, and proceeded to a village in order to give battle to the enemy. On learning that the chief of Alloo and his family had fled in a canoe, we returned to our canoes, made sail in pursuit of the chief, but did not overtake him. After returning and spending a day or two at the Island of Alloo, we launched our canoes and went to our respective homes, and heard no more of the war.

Some time after my master returned to the island where we usually resided, a canoe came and brought the information that a vessel was anchored near one of the head islands—that she carried guns on each side, and had a hundred men; and that they (the natives that brought the news) had been on board of the vessel, and received presents of beads, which they had on their necks. The natives said the vessel was not like our ship which we came on; but had only two masts. I told them we had vessels of all descriptions; some with one mast only. They said the men on board did not look like us, and that they were very saucy. I informed the natives the vessel was a war vessel, and that if molested by the natives, they would shoot them. The natives said they would take the vessel and kill all the men on board. I told them their safety consisted in friendship, that any hostile attack on the crew of the schooner would lead to their own destruction. They then set sail for Milly, to inform the chiefs of the arrival of the vessel at the head island. The chiefs of Milly gave orders to launch the canoes, fifteen in number, to go and take the schooner. These canoes were manned by 200 natives. My master's canoe not being in perfect repair, we could not join the party. On the night of the 25th of November, we saw several of the canoes returning towards the island where I was. From one of the canoes landed the high chief, who began to question me respecting the vessel. I told him I had not seen the vessel, and of course could not tell much about her; but that I expected she had come after me and Lay, and that she would have us. He then said he had better kill us both, and then there would be no one to tell that the natives had killed the rest of the crew. I told him that the people on board the schooner knew there were two alive, and if they killed us, the crew of the vessel would kill all the natives. This appeared to perplex his mind, and he shortly left me, and retired to rest.

On the next morning (26th) the chief again questioned me respecting the vessel; but I could give him no particular information, as I had not seen her. The natives then commenced knotting up leaves to enquire of their god, who, they said, would inform them what was best to be done. Towards night they departed, leaving me with my master, giving him strict orders not to let me go to the vessel, fearing that I should not only remain on board, but give information that my shipmates had been murdered. I was glad to see them depart, for I feared they would kill me. The reader can have but a faint idea of my feelings at that time, nor will I attempt to describe them.

Towards the close of the next day (27th) a canoe came to the island, which had been boarded by a boat from the schooner. The natives offered the men in the boat some cocoanuts, which they would not accept. The boat then proceeded towards the Island of Milly. The natives informed me that the men in the boat inquired after the men who were left there by the ship Globe; but they would not give any information where they were. The canoe left the island, and we went to rest. The next day passed without hearing anything of the schooner; but the day following (29th of November), as I was walking in the afternoon, I heard a dreadful outcry for Hussey. I ran to the hut to learn the cause, and to my unspeakable joy, I discovered that one of the schooner's boats was on the beach, waiting for me, the men all armed and equipped for battle. As I approached, the Lieutenant spoke to me and told me to come to him. I went and sat down by him. He asked me several questions, but my feelings were so overcome and agitated, that I know not whether I replied in English, or the language of the natives. While we were sitting together, the old man whom I had always called master, but who was now willing to be considered my servant, asked me if the white people were going to kill him. The Lieutenant inquired of me to know the purport of the old man's question; I told him he was afraid of being killed. The Lieutenant replied that he should not be hurt, if he behaved himself properly.

We then walked round the island, and I collected what few things I had; a musket, etc., and made preparations for our departure. My old master being unwilling to part with me, asked

permission to go with me. I spoke to the Lieutenant on the subject, and he readily consented.
We then set sail, accompanied by my master and
his son. We soon fell in with the second Lieutenant, in another boat, who informed us that all
the survivors of the Globe's crew were now
rescued. The boats soon lost sight of each other,
as night came on, and that in which I was, arrived at the island about 9 o'clock in the evening.
We landed, cooked supper, and anchored our
boat at a little distance from the shore for the
night.

The next morning (30th), we got under way,
accompanied by the other boat, beat to the windward, for the outside passage, and then ran
down to the schooner, and got alongside at 9
o'clock. I will leave it for the reader to picture
my feelings on entering once more on board of
an American vessel, after having been among un-
merciful savages twenty-two months. We soon
had some breakfast, after which my hair was
cut, which was of two years' growth, and I was

furnished with clothing, and remained on board till the next day.

From this date to the time of our arrival in the United States, all the important incidents and facts which transpired, will be found in the preceding pages, arranged from the journal kept by Lay.

After expressing my thanks to all who assisted to rescue us from savage bondage, and my gratitude to Heaven for a safe return to my friends and native land, I bid the reader a respectful farewell.

Mr. Hussey died off Cape Horn on his way home from another voyage he had been upon, in the ship Congress, of Nantucket, in the year 1829, being twenty-four years of age.

THE END.

A NEW HOUSE OF PUBLISHERS.

"Nearly two years ago Dr. Carlos Martyn and Mr. Charles F. Rideal, both men of ideas and enterprise, and both voluminous writers, established a business for the publication of their own works. Success has attended their efforts in a most marked degree, and now Mr. Rideal and his colleague are presenting books other than the efforts of their own pens in the same artistic letterpress and binding that have contributed to the success of their original undertaking. Hence the house known as the Abbey Press has been established, with agencies in London, Paris, Melbourne, and elsewhere. The Catalogue of this press containing the list of books now ready and in preparation shows the fine and high-class works which characterize the publications of this house."—*New York Times Saturday Review*.

SOME VERDICTS OF THE PRESS.

Makes one glad the Abbey Press has come into the field.—*The Book and Newsdealer*, San Francisco.

The Abbey Press catalogue includes many attractive titles of works now in stock as well as numerous fine high-class book: in preparation.—*Newspaperdom*, New York.

The Abbey Press, New York, is sending out some excellei. books, and is fast forging to the front and will take its place with the leading publishing houses of the metropolis.—*Atlanta Saturday Review*.

A publishing house that is becoming widely known for th excellence of its work.—*The Book World*, New York.

AUTHORS AND ARTISTS

Appleton, George.
Atherly, Robert Drew.
Ayr, Landis.
Barnes, Willis.
Bartz, U. S.
Borders, Joe H.
Brooke, Gregory.
Brown, Barnetta.
Buffington, T. P.
Burdick, Lewis Dayton.
Burling, Clinton Osgood.
Campbell, William M.
Cary, Katherine Miles.
Clark, William Adolphus.
Clarke, Albert G., Jr.
Clay, John M., Mrs.
Clemens, Will M.
Collins, Wilkie.
Cone, John A.
Craddock, Florence N.
Delanoy, M. Frances Hanford.
Dickens, Charles.
Doubleday, J. Stewart.
Drummond, Henry.
Duxbury, C. Richmond, Mrs.
Edwards, Almus Hugh.
Elshemus, L. M.
Emmel, May C.
Field, Elaine L.
Flattery, M. Douglas.
Fradenburgh, J. N.
French, Minnie Reid.
Fox, Page.
Gardner, Etta M.
Gardner, W. H.

Gordon, A. M. R.
Graham, Marie.
Green, Benjamin E.
Greenleaf, Sue.
Greer, Julian.
Gregory, Daniel Seelye.
Hamilton, Sam A.
Hammond, John Hays.
Harker, Charles R.
Harkins, James W., Jr.
Hartman, L. B.
Hartshorn, Mary A.
Hartt, Irene Widdemer.
Hobson, Margaret.
Holmes, Herbert.
Hopkins, Alphonso Alva.
Howard, Lady Constance.
Hussey, Cyrus M.
Hutchinson, Warren B.
Jennings, Edwin B.
Johnson, Stanley Edwards.
Johnston, Elizabeth Bryant.
Jokai, Maurus.
Kaven, E. Thomas.
Kearney, Belle.
Kellogg, J.
Kemble, W. Fretz.
Lawrence, William V.
Lay, William.
Lee, J. F.
Lindsay, Clarence M.
Loring, Mattie Balch.
Love, Margaret B.
Mackin, M.
Macleod, Warren M.

AUTHORS AND ARTISTS

Mankowski, De, Mary.
Marie, Rose.
Martin, Amarala.
Martin, Carlos.
Merimee, Prosper.
Middleton, E.
Miller, Andrew J.
Miller, Lischen M.
Milroy, Elizabeth.
Morris, James Edwin, Mrs.
Morris, Moses D.
Muir, Law.
Munn, Charles Clark.
Munyon, Dora Harvey.
Muzzy, Alice M.
Napoliello, R. R.
Niall, Mical Ui.
Nicholl, Edith M.
Nicolovius, Ludwig.
Ousley, Clarence.
Pacheco, Mary.
Palter, Emile A.
Pierson, Alice.
Pomeroy, Helen.
Preston, South G.
Pritchard, Agnes Camplejohn.
Raymond, Walter Marion.
Richard, Marie E.
Rideal, Charles F.
Riggs, Arthur Stanley.
Ripley, N. B.
Rogers, Charlotte Boardman.
Root, Frederick Stanley.
Rose, A. McGregor.
Roundy, Alice Miriam.
Rowe, C. H.

Runyan, N. P.
Sawyer, Nellie Tolman.
Scribner, Kimball.
Searle, E. W.
Seltzer, Charles A.
Simms, Margaret D.
Sheppard, Antoinette.
Smirnow, Louis.
Smith, Abbie N.
Smith, Howard T.
Stevenson, Robert Louis.
Stewart, M. B.
Stockwell, George A.
Stone, Isabel S.
Stormbrow, Harold.
Sutton, Warner P.
Tabor, Edward A.
Tobey, Olive C.
Tolstoy, Count.
Turner, E. R.
Valentine, Jane.
Van Rensselaer, J. K., Mrs.
Waite, Gertrude Mitchell.
Walker, Jessie.
Walker, Elliot.
Warren, H. V.
Weschcke, Emil.
Westervelt, Leonidas.
White, Elizabeth Stoughton Gale.
Williams, Benjamin W.
Wilson, Abbie Oliver.
Winbigler, Charles F.
Winter, C. Gordon.
Wright, W. H.
Young, Duncan F.
Young, G. L.

ADVERTISING AGENTS' DIRECTORY, THE.

Arranged alphabetically and in States, including Great Britain and Canada. Nothing of the kind has ever before appeared. All who for any reason wish to know who the advertising agents are and how they can be reached, will find the desired information here. The Directory is brought down strictly to date. Cloth. One Dollar. (In preparation.)

AFLOAT WITH OLD GLORY.

By H. V. Warren. This is a patriotic book, over which the Star-Spangled Banner floats, and from which, as though it were a man-of-war, the cannons thunder and the wild cheers of Uncle Sam's tars ring out far over the water. In these days of "wars and rumors of wars" such a book will be eagerly read. Cloth, 12mo. One Dollar.

AMERICAN ELOQUENCE.

By Carlos Martyn. A text book of oratory, with characteristic extracts, divided into passages suitable for declamation from the speeches of typical orators of all schools and sections from colonial times to the present day, together with brief personal sketches and critical estimates. Copious index. (In preparation.)

AMERICAN WOMEN OF THE TIME.

Being a Dictionary of Biographical Records of Eminent Living Women. Revised to date and edited by Mr. Charles F. Rideal, Mrs. John King Van Rensselaer and Dr. Carlos Martyn. It is the first time a book of reference of this kind has been compiled in the special interests of any women in any country. The efforts of the publishers will be directed towards the securing a standard work, founded on reliable data, and which will be a suitable addition to any bookshelf. Cloth. $7.50. (In preparation.)

BALLADS OF BROTHERHOOD.

By Alphonso Alva Hopkins. These poems are mighty with suppressed passion. As one reads them, the eye kindles and the pulse accelerates. The writer has broad sympathies and can say with the old Roman, "Nothing that concerns humanity is foreign to me." Cloth, small 12mo, 84 pages. Fifty Cents.

BEAUTIFUL HAND OF THE DEVIL, THE.

By Margaret Hobson. The plot and treatment in this novel bear out the striking and startling title. It will be read at a sitting. Cloth, small 12mo. Fifty Cents.

BOBTAIL DIXIE.

By Abbie N. Smith. Lovers of dogs (and their name is legion) have a treat in this book. The illustrations which accompany it speak as often and as loudly as the dog himself. Cloth, 12mo, profusely illustrated. One Dollar.

BRITANNIA; OR, THE WHITE QUEEN.

By the Rev. South G. Preston. An historical novel of rare power and absorbing interest, dealing with Queen Bess, Lord Bacon and other "high mightinesses" of the Elizabethan era. Cloth, 12mo. One Dollar.

CANDLE LIGHT, A, AND OTHER POEMS.

By Louis Smirnow. Poetry that appeals to the heart. Not the kind that is considered classical because it is stuffed with mythological subjects and with names of forgotten heroes. This proceeds from emotion and that intensity of feeling begotten only by experience, either direct or observed, and excites the same emotions and feelings in the readers. This is the mission of true poetry. Cloth. One Dollar.

CAT TALES IN VERSE.

By Elliot Walker. The multitudinous friends (young and old) of cats will welcome in this book an absolutely new thing under the sun, namely, the *miaous* of their favorites set in rhyme. Owners of cats and these feline animals themselves owe this author a unanimous vote of thanks. The verses are unique and admirably done. Cloth, with cover designed by C. H. Rowe. Fifty Cents.

CAVALIER POETS.

By Clarence M. Lindsay. These sketches of the poets of England about the period of the Commonwealth, are gems. They are full enough to give the much needed information, but yet so brief that they may be read with ease. Specimens of the style of each are given, and the reader in an hour or two can grasp knowledge which otherwise he cannot gain in as many weeks or months. Cloth, small 12mo. Fifty Cents.

CHRISTIAN SCIENCE AND KINDRED SUPERSTITIONS.

By the Rev. Charles F. Winbigler. Written on a polemical subject, yet in a kindly spirit. The arraignment of Mrs. Eddy is keen and incisive, and the basis of her so-called science is analyzed and overthrown with great good humor, but with remorseless logic. The best popular discussion of Christian Science now in the market. Specially commended to Church people and Sunday School librarians. Cloth, 12mo. One Dollar.

CHRIST'S MESSAGE TO THE CHURCHES.

By William M. Campbell. Of special interest to Biblical students. The exegesis is exceedingly clear and is always plausible, even when not entirely convincing. New light is thrown on old difficulties. The author will be sure of attracting thousands of interested readers. Cloth, 12mo, 170 pages. One Dollar.

COALS OF FIRE.

By M. Frances Hanford Delanoy. Those who have read Mrs. Delanoy's "Serious Complications," as well as those who have not, will eagerly seize upon this book. It is equally good in its way. The title gives the key to the contents of the book, which we will not deprive the reader of the pleasure of exploring by outlining the plot. Cloth, 12mo. One Dollar.

CONCHITA'S ANGELS.

By Agnes Camplejohn Pritchard. The first sketch, from which the book takes it title, deals with matters incident to the late Cuban war, patriotism, suffering, privation, tragedy. Pathos and humor are combined in three other stories which go to make up the book. Cloth, 12mo, 216 pages. One Dollar.

CONSPIRACY OF YESTERDAY, A.

By Mical Ui Niall. This story would please the Boers, since it depicts the discomfiture of England and the triumph of those who hate her. It must be remembered, however, that it is only a story. England still survives. Cloth, 12mo, daintily produced, 75 pages. Fifty Cents.

CONTINENTAL CAVALIER, A.

By Kimball Scribner. Author of "The Honor of a Princess" (twenty-third thousand), "The Love of the Princess Alice" (fifteenth thousand), and "In the Land of the Loon." The author writes here in his well-known popular style and contributes one more (and not the least) to the eagerly-awaited historical novels of Revolutionary times. His characters are resurrections and in them the past lives again. Mr. Kimball Scribner is rapidly becoming one of the most popular of the younger writers of to-day. With four illustrations on copper. Cloth, 12mo, 258 pages. One Dollar.

CORDELIA AND OTHER POEMS.

By N. B. Ripley. These verses are the work of a talented and scholarly clergyman, who has followed Sir Philip Sidney's recipe for poetry: "Look into thine own heart—and write." As a result, we have here thoughts that breathe and words that burn. Cloth, small 12mo. Fifty Cents.

COUNCIL OF THREE, THE.

By Charles A. Seltzer. A very interesting account of a supposed adventure in a romantic part of the world, together with a description of three remarkable characters grouped in a Council and governing an idyllic Commonwealth. The hero comes through safely and makes friends of the three councillors for life, thereby winning a fortune. Cloth, 12mo, 177 pages. One Dollar.

COUNTRY STORE WINDOW, A.

By Herbert Holmes. These poems ring true. They describe the thoughts and feelings of one gazing out upon life as through a country store window. The moral quality of the poems does not detract from, but rather enhances, their interest and value; while the literary form is unexceptionable. Cloth, 12mo. One Dollar.

CRIME OF CHRISTENDOM, THE.

By Daniel Seelye Gregory, L.D., LL.D. Here the Eastern Question is luminously described in its origin and development, by a master mind. It is by far the ablest and fullest discussion of the Turk in Europe extant. The work is scholarly and interesting, with photograph and biographical sketch of the author, and several maps. Cloth, 12mo, 330 pages. $1.50.

CROSS OF HONOR, THE.

By Charles F. Rideal and C. Gordon Winter. A military drama-lette in one act. The period is that of the Cuban war; the scene, the entrenchments at Santiago; the characters, five in number, are all masculine save one, who is a hospital nurse. It is very interesting and moves with military precision from the ringing up to the ringing down of the curtain. *Second Edition*. Daintily printed on Japanese paper and bound in stiff boards. One Dollar.

CURIOUS CASE OF GENERAL DELANEY SMYTHE, THE.

By W. H. Gardner, Lieutenant-Colonel U. S. A. (retired). Not for many years has a more interesting or mysterious story appeared than this. Those who follow the fortunes of General Delaney Smythe will certainly corroborate this statement. The book will have a wide and permanent sale. With four illustrations by Miss Lowenstein. Cloth, 12mo, specially designed cover, 204 pages. One Dollar.

DANGER SIGNALS FOR NEW CENTURY MANHOOD.

By Edward A. Tabor. Is a masterly discussion of the dangers that confront the individual as well as the society of to-day in the United States. It is also a beautiful portraiture of the young manhood which should exist in the 20th century. Including photograph and biographical sketch of the author. 12mo, cloth bound, 316 pages. One Dollar.

DAYS THAT ARE NO MORE, THE.

By Elizabeth Bryant Johnston. These are stories of the Old South. The author depicts scenes and characters which belong to the recent past, but yet which seem to be as remote as the days of the Crusades. It is fortunate that those familiar with "Dixie" before the war yet live to paint it before it fades forever out of view. Cloth, 12mo, daintily bound. One Dollar.

DEFEATED, BUT VICTOR STILL.

By William V. Lawrence. A story of the mysteries of New Orleans following the Civil War and during the period of Reconstruction. Nothing more interesting has been put on the market for a long time. *Second Edition.* Cloth, 12mo, 424 pages. One Dollar.

DEMOCRACY AND THE TRUSTS.

By Edwin B. Jennings, author of "People and Property." The author shows that there is an irrepressible conflict between these two. They are, or must soon be, locked in a deadly conflict, and if one is to survive, the other must perish. Mr. Jennings' style is trenchant, and his arraignment of trusts in the interest of democracy must be read to be appreciated. Cloth, 65 pages. Fifty Cents.

DEVOUT BLUEBEARD, A.

By Marie Graham. This is a keen, satirical story which hits off foibles and humbugs in religious administration; not in an infidel spirit, but by a friendly hand and from the inside; one is kept guessing who's who. Cloth, 12mo, 300 pages. One Dollar.

DOCTOR JOSEPHINE.

By Willis Barnes. A charming love story, interwoven with hints and suggestions as to how to harmonize the warring interests of capital and labor. The author thinks the secret of union lies in profit sharing. Cloth, 12mo. One Dollar.

DOCTRINE OF THE BOOK OF ACTS, THE.

By G. L. Young. The work of a scholarly and competent clergyman, who writes in a bright, unsectarian spirit, throwing light into every dark corner of this important portion of the New Testament. Men and women of all creeds will find here a careful and suggestive dissection of the teachings of the apostles in the formative period of the Christian Church. *Second Edition.* Cloth, 12mo. One Dollar.

DIABOLICAL IN SCRIPTURE AND IN HUMAN LIFE, THE.

By Harold Stormbrow, D.D., LL.D. A curious discussion of the existence, personality and activity of Satan as he appears in Holy Writ and in history, together with the opinions of eminent men in all walks of life, concerning his attributes and real character. Cloth, 8vo. Limited edition. Ten Dollars. (In preparation.)

DIP IN THE POOL, A.—(Bethesda.)

"The Whole World is Aweary." "Be Refreshed and Better." By Barnetta Brown. Our manner of thinking about matters and things has much more to do with our success and happiness than is usually admitted, and the little Bethesda Book seeks to suggest a train of thought which will refresh life's oft-time weary traveler. What more refreshing to the body than a dip in cool, cleansing water? So to the mind, strained, tired and puzzled, there is nothing more refreshing than a dip in a pool of freshening, strengthening, cleansing thought ; and this pool of clean thought this Sunshine Book makes a modest attempt to provide in one of the "Sunshine Books" which has the endorsement of the International Sunshine Society. Cloth (Miniature), daintily produced. Twenty-five Cents. The set of Six, $1.50.

DOOMED TURK, THE ;

or, The End of the Eastern Question. By E. Middleton. An interesting and striking discussion of the Eastern Question. It is a timely book. The eyes of the world are fastened upon the Orient, and what to do with the Chinaman in the far East and with the Turk in the nearer East are the questions of the hour. The author's suggested method of handling the latter question is as unique as it is original. Cloth. Fifty Cents.

EXPERIENCE.

"How to Take It: How to Make It." By Barnetta Brown. This booklet contains the *secret* many have been trying to discover, more or less consciously, for a long time ; and it is believed that if the method of *taking* experience, set forth, is faithfully followed, it will lead to a great deal of happiness, and later on to a certain and satisfactory way of *making* it. The unreasonable appearance of experience is made to assume its real and true proportions; and all who read it will see that reason instead of chaos, orderly sequence instead of disorder, in all forms of experience once duly appreciated as truth, will change darkness into brightness. One of the "Sunshine Books" which has the endorsement of the International Sunshine Society. Cloth (Miniature), daintily produced. Twenty-five Cents. The set of Six, $1.50.

FEATHER'S WEIGHT, A.
By Amarala Martin. This is a story of mystery—one of those breathless tales which hold the attention from the start to the finish. Unlike some of them, it ends as the reader would have it do, and at the close all goes merry as the marriage bell. *Second Edition.* Cloth, small 12mo, 131 pages. Fifty Cents.

FIGHTING AGAINST FATE.
By Moses D. Morris. An exciting and true story, more dramatic than a drama. Those who like a blood-curdling, hair-raising narrative which has the advantage of being fact instead of fiction, are recommended to buy this book. A large sale is already assured. Cloth, 12mo, 260 pages, with one hundred striking illustrations. One Dollar.

FLOWER OF THE TROPICS, A,
And Other Stories of Mexico and the Border. By Warner P. Sutton. This author, a distinguished diplomat and lawyer, who was also Consul-General in Mexico for ten years, gives in this work a number of extremely interesting sketches of Mexican and Border life. The stories are saturated with the Spanish spirit and with the genius of the localities described. Cloth, 12mo, 121 pages, daintily printed and bound. One Dollar.

FOUNDATION RITES.
By Lewis Dayton Burdick. The rites and ceremonies prevalent among barbarous and semi-barbarous peoples are reproduced in a modified form in all the higher civilizations. In this masterly work, the author traces the relations between the primitive beginnings and the later evolutions. Mr. Burdick has amassed a great treasure of facts and illustrations which he makes both interesting and instructive. Cloth, 12mo. $1.50.

FROM CLOUDS TO SUNSHINE;
or, The Evolution of a Soul. By E. Thomas Kaven. Author of "A Duel of Wits," etc. Those who enjoy a luminous discussion of current questions relating to the origin and age of man, etc., conducted in a most finished manner, will find a treat in this volume. It is full of snap, vim and good humor. Cloth, 12mo, 182 pages. One Dollar.

FROM THE FOUR WINDS.
By Warren B. Hutchinson. These poems are vigorous productions, full of power, and throb with true poetic feeling. The poet touches upon many themes within a small space, and always suggestively as well as melodiously. Cloth, small 12mo. Fifty Cents.

GLOBE MUTINY, THE.

By William Lay, of Saybrook, Conn., and Cyrus M. Hussey, of Nantucket, the only survivors from the massacre of the ship's company by the natives. A narrative of the mutiny on board the ship "Globe," of Nantucket, in the Pacific Ocean, January, 1824, and the journal of a residence of two years on the Mulgrave islands, with observations on the manners and customs of the inhabitants. A most entertaining reprint of a work published in 1828. This book is a cross between one of Russell Clark's sea stories and "Robinson Crusoe." It deals with a real case of mutiny and the narrative is entrancing. It will be read with absorbing interest by all lovers of sea stories. Cloth, 12mo, 163 pages. Seventy-five Cents.

GREAT BREAD TRUST, THE.

By W. H. Wright. This booklet paints a supposed trust in bread, after the example of the Standard Oil Company, and which is owned and managed by a little group of multi-millionaires. Although the case is supposed, it outlines a condition of things which may well be apprehended and sounds a note of alarm in advance. Cloth, Miniature Series, 54 pages. Fifty Cents.

GREATEST THING IN THE WORLD, THE.

By Henry Drummond. Cloth, with photograph and biographical sketch of the author. Fifty Cents.

GREEN VALLEY.

By T. P. Buffington. Opening with a robbery, this novel ends with a marriage. Between the starting point and the end, a variety of interesting and exciting episodes are found. The scene is laid in the South and characteristic occurrences are related. The moral is wholesome and the hero and heroine are happy at last, as they deserve to be. Cloth, 12mo, 151 pages. One Dollar.

HALF HOUR STORIES.

By Dora Harvey Munyon. The stories are admirably told and each successive one seems a little better than the previous tale. The author writes with remarkable insight and describes life with rare fidelity. Cloth, 12mo, 148 pages. One Dollar.

HANDFUL OF RHYMES, A.

By Lischen M. Miller. This book of poems has an interest through the unusual merit of the verses. It is often said that this is not a poetical age, but the singer of to-day finds sufficient material and readers enough to make it clear that the question is open to debate. Cloth, 12mo. $1.50.

HEART'S DESIRE, THE.

"The Moth for the Star; The Night for the Morrow." By Barnetta Brown. That there is really only one desire, this Sunshine Book contends; that all desire can be truly and lastingly satisfied in our life, in other than the way it indicates, this little book denies. Some may not agree at once; but, sooner or later, the chord in the heart will be touched, and in the vibration will be caught the echo of "Home, Sweet Home." To read it, is finally to believe. To believe, is to work towards the end in view. To reach this is the consummation and the height of earthly happiness. One of the "Sunshine Books" which has the endorsement of the International Sunshine Society. Cloth (Miniature), daintily produced. Twenty-five Cents. The set of Six, $1.50.

✓ HEROINE OF SANTIAGO, THE;

or, What Followed the Sinking of the Merrimac. By Antoinette Sheppard. One of the very best of the many stories suggested by the Spanish—American war. The heroine is a lovable creature and after passing through many adventures—but we will not reveal the dénoûment. There is not a dull page in the whole book. Cloth, 12mo. One Dollar.

✓ HOCH DER KAISER.

Myself und Gott. By A. McGregor Rose (A. M. R. Gordon). This is the remarkable poem, which made a sensation in two hemispheres, and the recital of which by an American naval officer at a dinner nearly cost him his captaincy and embroiled the United States with Germany. It is here presented with appropriate and striking original illustrations by Miss Jessie A. Walker. It is a work of art. Cloth, 12mo, striking cover. Fifty Cents.

HOW TO ENJOY MATRIMONY;

or, The Monogamic Marriage Law Amended by Trial-Expiration Clause. By Rose Marie. An interesting and unique discussion of a subject of universal interest and concern. The author's conclusions may or may not commend themselves to every one, but her arguments are singularly able, and will stir thought and discussion. Cloth. Twenty-five Cents.

HOW TOMMY WAS CURED OF CRYING.

By Gertrude Mitchell Waite. This story will please children mightily; as also will the illustrations. Both are exceedingly well done. There could be no more fitting gift than this dainty and attractive book. Cloth, fully illustrated and daintily produced. Fifty Cents.

13

HOUSE OF A TRAITOR, THE.
By Prosper Merimée. With photograph and biographical sketch of the author. Cloth. Fifty Cents.

INTELLECTUAL PEOPLE.
By William Adolphus Clark. All readers are, or wish to be thought, intellectual people, hence this little work makes a universal appeal. It is one of the most piquant and suggestive discussions imaginable. The fact that it has gone in such a short time into a third edition proves that it has received merited recognition. *Third Edition.* Cloth, daintily produced, small 12mo, 97 pages. Fifty Cents.

INTERNATIONAL DIRECTORY OF AUTHORS, THE.
With a full list of the titles of their works, dates of publication, etc. Compiled and edited by Charles F. Rideal and Carlos Martyn.
(In preparation.)

IRON HAND, THE.
By Howard T. Smith. The department store, a comparatively new field, is exploited in this novel. The multitudes who are employed in these places and the vaster multitudes who shop in in them, will alike be interested in this story. Evidently the author writes from behind the scenes and knows whereof he affirms. The book will make a sensation. Cloth, 12mo. Illustrated. One Dollar.

JONAS BRAND;
or, Living Within the Law. By Jane Valentine. A book which shows how brutal a man may be in his domestic relations and still escape from all legal penalties. The story is well told and the characters are depicted with rare skill. The author is an adept in working a plot up to a thrilling climax. *Second Edition.* Cloth, 12mo, well printed and bound, 263 pages. One Dollar.

KEY-WORDS AND PHRASES OF THE NEW TESTAMENT.
By the Rev. South G. Preston. A very important and suggestive help in the study of the New Testament. Instead of having to search these out for himself, the reader is supplied with them without effort on his part. The book is a great labor saver. 56 chapters, 324 pages, 45 leading words and phrases of the New Testament, critically examined.

"Even in the region of that which is familiar to scholars he has shed much light."—JNO. J. TIGERT, D.D.

A rare book of information and very suggestive. *Second Edition.* Cloth, 12mo. One Dollar.

14

LIFE'S SPRINGTIME.

By J. N. Fradenburgh. Essays descriptive of the period of youth and full of wholesome and inspiring advice to those of both sexes who stand upon the threshold of life. Elders looking for something to place in the hands of the thoughtful and ambitious among the upcoming generation will find here exactly what they seek. Cloth, 12mo. One Dollar.

LIQUID FROM THE SUN'S RAYS.

By Sue Greenleaf. The theory suggested in this book is striking, yet seems workable. Those who are interested in new ideas suggestively and plausibly stated are recommended to look into the matters which are herein exploited. Cloth, 12mo. One Dollar.

LITERARY LIFE.

The most popular magazine for authors, publishers, booksellers and every one interested in literature, issued. It is a thoroughly impartial journal, readable from cover to cover. Five Cents per copy or Fifty Cents per annum, mailed free.

LITTLE COURT OF YESTERDAY, A.

By Minnie Reid French. A Virginia story of rare interest and merit. It concerns the grand passion and works itself out through strange vicissitudes to a satisfactory ending. The work is unusually dainty and attractive. Cloth, 12mo, 232 pages. One Dollar.

LITTLE SCARECROW, THE.

By Maurus Jokai. With photograph and biographical sketch of the author. Cloth. Fifty Cents.

LODGING IN THE NIGHT, A.

By Robert Louis Stevenson. This is the first time that this celebrated story has been produced in a manner worthy of the reputation of its talented author. It will be issued in a most dainty binding, forming a unique gift book. With photograph and biographical sketch of the author. Cloth. Fifty Cents.

LOST LOUISIANA, THE.

By J. Kellogg. An historical romance dealing with gold and silver mines worked by the Spaniards in the old Louisiana territory, and hence so named, but lost for many years. An interesting story is told in connection with these mines, and some important truths are advocated. Cloth, 12mo. One Dollar.

15

LOVE AND PRIDE.

By R. R. Napoliello. This novel admirably portrays the play and counterplay of master passions. The hero, an Italian, bares his soul to inspection, so that we see and participate in the struggle. A rare psychological study. Cloth. Fifty Cents.

LOVE'S RANDOM SHOT.

By Wilkie Collins. With photograph and biographical sketch of the author. Cloth. Fifty Cents.

MAGISTRACY, THE.

Being a Directory and Biographical Dictionary of the Justices of the Peace of the United States. Compiled and edited by Charles F. Rideal and Carlos Martyn. (In preparation.)

MAN WITHOUT THE OATH, THE.

By Olive C. Tobey. This is a breathless story and the reader pants as he reads, as though he had been walking fast, or running, and lays the book down with a sigh of regret because it is not longer. The characters are varied and lifelike; the adventures are manifold and the dialogue is crisp and sparkling. Cloth, 12mo, fully illustrated. One Dollar.

MASTER AND MAN.

By Count Tolstoy. With photograph and biographical sketch of the author. Cloth. Fifty Cents.

MEN, WOMEN, AND LOVING.

"With an Eye Made Quiet, We See Into the Heart of Things." By Barnetta Brown. Men think they know all about loving and so do women; but judging from the general appearance of loving and its often unsatisfying results, some things in regard to it have apparently been forgotten, or, for some unaccountable reason, hidden deeply away. Reminders are useful, on occasion, and a gentle jog of the elbow sometimes saves one from falling into error; and if this little book serves the purpose of straightening out a jumble in any affair of the heart, or leads man or woman to a true, brave thought of loving, it will have made its excuse for existence. One of the "Sunshine Books" which has the endorsement of the International Sunshine Society. Cloth (Miniature), daintily produced. Twenty-five Cents. The set of Six, $1.50.

MISS PENELOPE'S ELOPEMENT,

and Other Stories. By Katherine Miles Cary. These sketches are very vivacious. The style is colloquial and the book reads as though the best of story tellers was seated at our side and favoring us with an oral recitation. Cloth, small 12mo. Fifty Cents.

16

MISTAKES OF AUTHORS, THE.

A Manual for Writers and Others. Being a treatise on Bulls, Blunders, Mistakes, Errors, Literary Anachronisms and Misfits. Edited by Will M. Clemens, author of "A Ken of Kipling," "The Depew Story Book," "The Life of Theodore Roosevelt," "Life of Admiral Dewey," "The Mark Twain Story Book," "The Choate Story Book," etc., etc. Limited autograph edition. Cloth, 12mo. One Dollar.

MISTRESS OF MANY MOODS, A.

By Charlotte Boardman Rogers. This book, in the French of André Theuriet, made a sensation. Miss Rogers' translation is admirable and preserves the vivacity and spirit of the original with lifelike fidelity. It is no less interesting in the English than in the French version. Cloth, small 12mo. Fifty Cents.

MYSTERY OF THE MARBLETONS, THE;

A Romance of Reality. By M. Mackin. Stories of mystery are always popular. This is one of the best of its kind, and holds the reader breathless from the first page to the last. The interest steadily increases to the end. This book is certain to be widely read. Cloth, small 12mo, daintily produced. Fifty Cents.

NARRAGANSETT PEER, A.

By George Appleton. A romance of Southern New England founded upon fact. The heir to a great property is made a prisoner while his relatives riot in his wealth. He is discovered by two newspaper reporters, and the incidents of the prisoner's release and return to his own, make an interesting story often pathetic and humorous. Cloth, 12mo. One Dollar.

NEW DON QUIXOTE, THE.

By Mary Pacheco. The hero of this book is a Western ranchman who suddenly finds himself heir to an earldom in England, and who takes among the conventionalities of the Old Country the breezy freedom of the prairies and the land of Uncle Sam. Cloth 12mo. Specially designed cover by C. H. Rowe. One Dollar.

NEW ENGLAND FOLK.

By Mrs. C. Richmond Duxbury. A strong, realistic novel of the best modern type. It abounds in incident, while the characters are sketched with the vigorous hand of a master. The plot is well conceived and the local color is one of the strong features of the book. Cloth, 12mo 295 pages. One Dollar.

17

NEW SWISS FAMILY ROBINSON, THE.

By Helen Pomeroy. This is a new "Swiss Family Robinson." Without being a copy of that famous work, it nevertheless suggests it and is full of the same kind of realism and adventure. Young people will here find a feast. Cloth, 12mo. One Dollar.

NEW VERSION OF AN OLD STORY, A.

By Elizabeth Milroy. A charming tale told in melodious verse, with a most helpful and inspiring dénouement. A farmer and his wife change work, and the man gets a new conception of the meaning and importance of housework and is glad enough to return to the field. Daintily produced. Twenty-five Cents.

N'TH FOOT IN WAR, THE.

By Lieut. M. B. Stewart, U. S. Army. This is a plain unvarnished tale, descriptive of the daily life of a soldier in the United States Army. It traces his experiences throughout the day and night, showing exactly what he is, how he feels and acts, what he eats and where he sleeps. The book is of deep interest as a faithful portraiture of "the man behind the gun." Cloth, 12mo. Attractively designed cover. One Dollar.

OCTAVIA, THE OCTOROON.

By J. F. Lee. In this story we have a setting forth of the old relations between the blacks and whites down in "Dixie," with a suggestion of the sexual questions involved in, and evolved from, the said relations. The interest is sustained and the book will find many readers. Cloth. Fifty Cents.

ODD JEWEL, AN.

A Postnuptial Tale of a World-wide Passion. By Warren M. Macleod. This is a prose poem. It deals with the unhappy loves of a hero and heroine worthy of a better fate, but who were separated at first by the machinations of a false friend and afterwards by death. Cloth, small 12mo, 159 pages. Fifty Cents.

OLD GRAHAM PLACE, THE.

By Etta M. Gardner. Is a story of home life. It illustrates the power of a resourceful woman in a trying crisis and proves that "an appeal to arms" is not the most effective way of solving domestic problems, and that victory often lies in wait for the one who laughs. The characters are vividly sketched and the story abounds in attractive situations and delicate humor. Effective use has been made of the element of chance in bringing about the dénoûment. Viewed as a whole, the story is most fascinating. Cloth. Fifty Cents.

OLD SCHOOL DAYS.

By Andrew J. Miller. This book should have a wide reading. It is healthy and breezy with youth and sport. In its pages the experiences of all of us are laughably and vividly recalled. Cloth, 12mo, attractively designed. 248 pages. One Dollar.

ONE THOUSAND WAYS TO MAKE MONEY.

By Page Fox. Every man, woman, boy and girl should read this book. It conveys information of use to every one, and will enable those who read it to make an honest livelihood in dozens of unthought-of ways. *Second Edition.* Cloth, 12mo, 331 pages. One Dollar.

ON THE CHARLESTON.

By Irene Widdemer Hartt. The smell of the sea and the odors of the woods and fields of Guam are in these pages. The tale sways, like the ocean swell, between Jack Tar and the soldiers in the Yanko-Spanko War. Cloth, 12mo, 289 pages. One Dollar.

ON THE THRESHOLD;

A Hillside Sketch. By Mary A. Hartshorn. Dealing, as this book does, with the morning of life, it has the charm of the dawn, the sparkle of the dewdrops and the general freshness incidental to the season with which it deals. It is a poem in prose, and must be read to be appreciated. Daintily produced. Twenty-five Cents.

OUR CHOIR.

By George A. Stockwell. The experiences of a church choir, harmonious and inharmonious, sung in diminuendo and crescendo, together with airs major (ity) and minor (ity) heard from the congregation, are voiced in this amusing and entertaining brochure. Those who have heard and seen church choirs (who has not?) will read this book with gusto. *Second Edition.* Cloth, 12mo, 83 pages. Fifty Cents.

PAIR OF KNAVES AND A FEW TRUMPS, A.

By M. Douglas Flattery. The literary quality of this fascinating novel would alone call attention to it. When to this are added plots and counterplots, dramatic contests and dénoûments, the book presents a combination of attractions quite unique and irresistible. Mr. Flattery's books, as, for example, " Wife or Maid ?" are always readable and interesting. Cloth, 12mo, fully illustrated, 310 pages. One Dollar.

PACIFIC COAST VACATION, A.

By Mrs. James Edwin Morris. The views and experiences of a traveler who goes pleasuring across the continent and minutely explores the Pacific Coast, are here recorded with great skill and power. Salient points are strongly emphasized and the book is a *vade mecum*, which all travelers can use to advantage. Cloth, 12mo, beautifully illustrated. One Dollar.

PEOPLE AND PROPERTY.

By Edwin B. Jennings. An animated, logical discussion of the question of corporate rights versus human rights. Lincoln said that "when a dollar comes in conflict with a man he sided with the man." This book is timely, able and interesting. Cloth. Fifty Cents.

PHARAOH.

By Mary De Mankowski. This translation, an abridgment of one of the most popular foreign stories of the day, is a new triumph for the author whose former translation, "Ten Years in Cossack Slavery," has made such a sensation. That was a narrative ; this is a novel descriptive of life in ancient Egypt. While a story, it yet possesses an historical basis and gives many curious incidents connected with the life of the Pharaohs. Cloth, 12mo. $1.25.

PITTED AGAINST ANARCHISTS.

By W. Fretz Kemble. A chief of police in an imaginary State gives herein his thrilling adventures in contending with and finally circumventing a number of Anarchists, who killed one king and were plotting to destroy his successor. The novel reads like a record from headquarters, and a remarkable air of verisimilitude pervades the story. Cloth, 12mo, 118 pages. Fifty Cents.

POCKET ISLAND.

A Story of Country Life in New England. By Charles Clark Munn. A remarkably attractive book written in a remarkably attractive manner. With frontispiece. Cloth, 12mo, fully illustrated, 200 pages. *Third and Revised Edition.* One Dollar.

PRAIRIE FLOWER, A.

By Alice Pierson. There are many flowers upon the prairie, both natural and human, but among them all the blossom described in this book bears the palm. She is as sweet as her name and as deserving as she is sweet. Cloth, small 12mo, 88 pages. Fifty Cents.

PRIEST AND A WOMAN, A.

By Landis Ayr. This is a story of breathless interest, which terminates in an unexpected dénoûment. The lights and shades, the interplay of contrasts, the incidents of the story, are the work of a masterhand in fiction. A previous novel by this writer attained wide celebrity. Cloth, 12mo, 268 pages, designed cover. One Dollar.

PRINCE OF THE EAST, A.

By James W. Harkins, Jr. This is an East Indian story of rare and thrilling interest. It is steeped in Oriental atmosphere and transports the reader, like the prince on his Oriental carpet, to the scenes and experiences described. Lovers of the occult will be delighted with it. Cloth, 12mo, 324 pages, finely bound. One Dollar.

PSYCHOLOGY OF THE NEW TESTAMENT, THE.

By the Rev. South G. Preston. A careful, comprehensive, scholarly study of a most important and interesting subject. This work is indispensable to all students of Holy Writ and of human nature. Clergymen will find it a mine of suggestive information. Cloth, 12mo. One Dollar.

PUPPET SHOW, THE.

By Leonidas Westervelt. This new edition is a considerable improvement upon the former one in matter, and especially in mechanical form. The novel is the work of a clever young writer. It gives an inside view of society. *Second and Revised Edition.* Cloth, 12mo, 219 pages. One Dollar.

QUAKER SCOUT, A.

By N. P. Runyan. The contradictory title adopted by Mr. Runyan piques curiosity, which, upon investigation, will be abundantly rewarded. Incidents without number succeed one another in rapid and romantic succession, making the reader hold his breath in sympathy with the recital. Cloth, 277 pages. $1.25.

QUEEN OF APPALACHIA, THE.

By Joe H. Borders. Dealing with Western scenes and characters, this novel is as breezy and invigorating as the prairie itself. The hero is a queer genius. We venture to say that there is no book exactly like this now in the market. Cloth, 12mo. One Dollar.

RACE WITH A HURRICANE, A.

By Alice Miriam Roundy. The story which gives the title to this book is of the hurricane order and blows the heroine into a port of peace at last. The other stories making up the volume are all equally interesting and concern various topics. Considerable versatility is shown by the author. Cloth, small 12mo, 101 pages. Fifty Cents.

ROMANCE AND ROME.

By Almus Hugh Edwards. This is a booklet which gives in a small compass a vast deal of interesting information regarding the Eternal City, past and present. The descriptive parts are strung together on a delightful thread of romance in the shape of a little love story. Cloth, small 12mo, 103 pages. Fifty Cents.

ROMANCE IN MEDITATION, A.

By Elaine L. Field. A dainty and charming portraiture of a maiden's ideal evolved in a series of meditations, only to be rudely shattered at last. The book is unique both in conception and in execution. Cloth, small 12mo. Fifty Cents.

REPUBLIC OF AMERICA, THE.

By L. B. Hartman. A timely work, full of patriotic inspiration. The author depicts the martial side of American life with militant power and shows that good soldiers are indispensable factors of aggressive civilization. In view of the recent Spanish-American war, of the situation in the Philippines and of the disturbance in China, no book could be more timely. *Second Edition*. Cloth, 12mo, 116 pages. Fifty Cents.

SECRET OF HAMLET, THE.

By the Rev. South G. Preston. An intensely interesting analysis of this enigmatical character and a new solution of the Hamlet problem. The book is both scholarly and unusual. *Second Edition*. Cloth, 12mo. One Dollar.

SERIOUS COMPLICATIONS.

By M. Frances Hanford Delanoy. This book is a rollicking comedy, full of delicate satire and laughable situations. Its dramatic possibilities are unbounded. Indeed, it has been produced as a comedy and lends itself to such treatment in every sentence. The dialogue is crisp, the movement swift, and the dénoûement quite unexpected, although natural. Cloth, 12mo, 196 pages, with eight full page illustrations, daintily produced. One Dollar.

SHADOW OF THE KING, THE.

By the Rev. South G. Preston. This is a book of a devotional character. It blends in a rare and successful way spirituality and interest—one of the most difficult things to do. It leaves a sweet taste in the mouth. *Second Edition.* Cloth, 12mo. One Dollar.

SHAKESPEARE AND GOETHE ON GRESHAM'S LAW AND THE SINGLE GOLD STANDARD.

By Benjamin E. Green. This is a suggestive work in which the historian, the statesman, the politician, the banker, the business man and working man will find much food for thought, mixed with some refreshing gossip for the general reader.

SINGULAR SINNER, A.

By Charles R. Harker. The alliterative title of this novel is significant of the subject and of its treatment. The hero is a gentleman robber, whose adventures are as romantic as those of Dick Turpin or Claude Duval of old. Cloth, 12mo. One Dollar.

SLAVEHOLDER'S DAUGHTER, A.

By Belle Kearney. Full of Southern life and character, and readable from cover to cover. With 11 full-page illustrations and frontispiece. Cloth, 12mo, 270 pages. One Dollar.

SOCIAL SINNERS.

A realistic novel of to-day. By Emile A. Palier. Portrays a number of Sinners and a few Saints in the modern social order. Certain passages hold the reader spellbound. There are several heroes and heroines, all true to life after their respective kind. Cloth, 12mo, 229 pages. One Dollar.

SOUL GROWTH.

"To Become or Not to Become; That is Your Question." By Barnetta Brown. To DO was the preaching and the teaching of the ancient order. To BE is the greater and the later endeavor. "Soul Growth" indicates a way by which people may become. The way may have been mentioned before, but this little book brings home to us once more, in very simple fashion, an old, old story. Applied closely to everyday life, the thought of this book will bring into this gray, old world more real sunshine than it has ever yet seen. One of the "Sunshine Books" which has the endorsement of the International Sunshine Society. Cloth, (Miniature), daintily produced. Twenty-five Cents, The set of Six, $1.50.

SOLDIER'S REVENGE, THE;

or, Roland and Wilfred. By Florence N. Craddock. This is a novel which describes cadet life at West Point in a most realistic and entertaining manner. In these military days, when wars and rumors of wars are in the air, such a book deserves and should have a wide reading. Cloth, 12mo. One Dollar.

SOME PEOPLE WE MEET.

By Charles F. Rideal. A series of brightly written character sketches or types including "The Saleslady," "The Man 'Wot' Golfs," "Won Lung Lee," "The Rev. Hiram B. Montgomery," "Jackie," "Bob Toughun," "A City 'Gent,'" "Mr. Levi Vindermenderheimer," "Mr. Tammany Todd," "Mr. Sempronious Yardly," "Mr. Dick Drummerton," "Mrs. Whirlingay Whiz." Miss Jessie A. Walker has provided pictures exhibiting her usual clever talent. Cloth, 12mo. Decorated Cover. Twenty-five Cents.

SOUR SAINTS AND SWEET SINNERS.

By Carlos Martyn. This is a portrait of some unsaintly saints and some unsinful sinners, who are types to be found in all churches and congregations, by a prominent clergyman who writes from the inside with a pen borrowed from Dean Swift. *Third Edition.* Cloth, 12mo, 245 pages with photograph and biographical sketch of the author. One Dollar.

STRANGER, THE.

By Mattie Balch Loring. These dainty verses show decided poetic and literary power. They cover a wide range of experience and observation, and run "from grave to gay, from lively to severe." Unlike much of the poetry of the day, what Mrs. Loring has written is likely to be long-lived. Cloth, 12mo, beautifully printed and bound. One Dollar.

STUDIES IN ESCHATOLOGY.

By U. S. Bartz. Biblical students are especially commended to this work. It gives in a brief and popular style a careful and scholarly view of the great subject of Eschatology, on the subjects of death, resurrection, immortality and the final judgment. Cloth, small 12mo, 86 pages. Fifty Cents.

SUNSHINE BOOKS.

By Barnetta Brown. Experience. Soul Growth. The Heart's Desire. Men, Women and Loving. Worry and Cheer. A Dip in the Pool. Cloth, daintily produced, 25 Cents each; Six in a set, (neatly boxed), $1.50.

SWEETBRIER.

By L. M. Elshemus. A story of sentimental and artistic interest. The hero has the soul of a poet and his verses are scattered throughout the book. The characters speak and act in keeping with their surroundings and interest the reader. Cloth, 12mo. Illustrated by the author. One Dollar.

TEMPER CURE, THE.

By Stanley Edwards Johnson. In the guise of a novel, the author gives a fanciful account of a cure for bad temper. There are no dull pages in this book. Cloth. Fifty Cents.

TEN YEARS IN COSSACK SLAVERY.

By Mary D. Mankowski. This is a graphic, thrilling description of the personal experiences of a patriotic Pole, condemned to Siberia for loving his country "not wisely but too well." The book explains the existing hatred of the Russian government and gives the reasons therefore. Cloth, 230 pages. $1.25.

TOBACCO SMOKE.

By Clarence Ousley. These verses, written in various moods and on many themes, are all steeped in the aroma of the fragrant weed and are the outcome of its inspiration. Every devotee of Nicotine, when bowing at that shrine, will use this dainty book as a litany. The author is a true poet. Fully and beautifully illustrated. Cloth, small 12mo. Fifty Cents.

TOM HUSTON'S TRANSFORMATION.

By Margaret B. Love. This is the story of a man who was jilted, and, as a result, became a drummer instead of a lawyer, but who, later meeting the right woman, was redeemed, regenerated and disinthralled, and regained his place among manly and honorable men. The story shows the power, both for good and evil, of womankind, and carries a wholesome moral. *Second Edition.* Cloth, small 12mo, 92 pages. Fifty Cents.

THROUGH STRESS AND STORM.

By Gregory Brooke. A strong, vigorous delineation of the tender passion which is sure to win wide favor. The hero, in his strength and weakness, is a type familiar to all. The heroine, as usual, is far superior to him in decision of character and is a lovable creation. Cloth, 12mo, specially designed cover. One Dollar.

TRANSVAAL TROUBLE, THE.

By John Hays Hammond. An American view of the British-Boer War in South Africa. The author is a financial magnate, thoroughly familiar with the whole subject by personal residence in the Transvaal, who speaks with authority because he knows whereof he speaks. Cloth. Twenty-five Cents.

TRAVELS OF A WATER DROP, THE.

By Mrs. James Edwin Morris. Is a volume of sketches, studies from nature. The travels and adventures of this particular Water Drop are so interestingly written that it ought to occupy a prominent place in children's classics. Each sketch in the book is a gem in its way. For scientific accuracy and literary beauty this little volume is recommended to nature lovers. Cloth, small 12mo. Fifty Cents.

TRIPLE FLIRTATION, A.

By L. M. Elshemus. This author is a prominent artist as well as a literary man. The illustrations alone are worth more than the price of the book, while the stories abound in interesting and exciting incidents. The characters are as well drawn as the pictures. Cloth, 12mo, 260 pages. Illustrated by the author. One Dollar.

TWENTY-FIVE MINUTES WITH PALMISTRY.

By Julian Greer. The subject here treated is popular. Extensive and expensive books on the subject abound. This work is intended to supply the demand for something brief and cheap, yet is sufficiently complete and thorough to put the reader in possession of all the necessary data for understanding and practising the science. Daintily produced. Cloth. Twenty-five Cents.

TWO MEN AND SOME WOMEN.

By Walter Marion Raymond. Two contrasting characters are described in this novel in a graphic and interesting way, together with their mutual influence over one another, and over certain women with whom they are brought in contact. It is a realistic story. Cloth, 12mo, 160 pages. One Dollar.

UNCLE PHIL.

By Mrs. John M. Clay. A Southern story, strong and absorbing. It describes the devotion of an old darkey "uncle" to the person and fortune of the heroine, who has a hard time of it, but who is at last brought safely to the shore largely through the self-sacrificing exertions of this faithful retainer. *Second and Revised Edition.* Cloth, 12mo. One Dollar.

26

UNO WHO.

By Elizabeth Stoughton White. A unique novel whose characters are wholly original. The scenes are laid partly here and partly abroad, while a charming love story runs through the tale, unifying and vitalizing every page. The element of romance is pronounced in this book. Cloth, 12mo. One Dollar.

VENGEANCE OF THE MOB, THE.

By Sam A. Hamilton. An exciting story of Florida, in which the characteristics and the effects of "Judge Lynch's" rule are exploited. A thrilling love story runs through the novel, with which the vengeance of the mob comes into collision. Cloth, 12mo, 206 pages. One Dollar.

VERANA.

By Emil Weschcke. A novel descriptive of adventures on the frontier. It depicts a new, strange life to those who dwell in the older and longer settled portions of the country, and will be read through at a single sitting by all readers who once begin it. Cloth, small 12mo. Fifty Cents.

WANTED—A MAN.

By Robert Drew Atherly. A charming story charmingly told. Both hero and heroine are bewitching creations, poetic and idyllic. Indeed this whole novel is a prose poem. Cloth, small 12mo. Fifty Cents.

WHAT IS THE MATTER WITH THE CHURCH?

By Frederick Stanley Root. Mr. Root seems to have borrowed the pen of Junius. He deals with pessimistic facts in an optimistic spirit. While sharply indicating the traditional Church, he shows that "faithful are the wounds of a friend." There are earthquakes in this book and upheavals of thought and action. Cloth, 12mo, 188 pages. One Dollar.

WHEN AT HOME AND SOCIETY GUIDE.

Giving Days when "At Home" of the Upper Classes. Compiled and edited by Charles F. Rideal. To which is added a chapter on the Etiquette of Calls and Calling, by Lady Constance Howard. Each Season. (In preparation.)

WIDOW ROBINSON, THE, AND OTHER SKETCHES.

By Benjamin W. Williams. These sketches, the first of which gives the title of the book, are admirable silhouettes of experience in life. They are deftly done and carry a wholesome and inspiring lesson. Cloth, small 12mo. Fifty Cents.

WHITE MAN'S CHANCE, THE.

By Abbie Oliver Wilson. In view of the continued lynchings in Dixie, this novel, which exploits the relations which might and should exist between the whites and the blacks, is both timely and significant. It is strongly written and carries a wholesome moral. Cloth, 12mo. One Dollar.

WITH A POLICEMAN IN SOUTH AFRICA.

By E. W. Searle. A true narrative of personal experiences in connection with the mounted police in Natal. It reads like a novel. The strange and, until recently, unknown country herein exploited is now the focus of all eyes. This is another contribution to a general knowledge of South Africa. Cloth, 12mo. Beautifully illustrated. Seventy-five Cents.

WOMAN'S REVENGE, A.

By Law Muir. This is a love story, with lurid accompaniments, the scene being laid in California. The characters are sharply drawn. The young wife, soon widowed, is betrayed by a wealthy rascal, upon whom she wreaks her vengeance. She is revenged, but in a strange and unexpected way. Cloth, small 12mo, 87 pages. Fifty Cents.

WORRY AND CHEER.

"The Way of Worry," "The Way of Cheer." By Barnetta Brown. This little book cheerfully undertakes to encourage the wanderers along life's pathway. Only too often are they met with, discouraged, dejected, sore of foot and bruised in heart The author, firmly believing that to make this journey a dismal one, is a very mistaken proceeding, as well as a very unnecessary one, endeavors to point out an agreeable and pleasant route. The broad gauge road of pleasantness, cheer and courage is recommended in preference to the opposition line and narrow gauge road of worry, anxiety and pain. One of the "Sunshine Books," which has the endorsement of the International Sunshine Society. Cloth. (Miniature), daintily produced. Twenty-five Cents. The set of Six, $1.50.

ADDENDA.

ARICKAREE TREASURE, THE.

By Albert G. Clarke, Jr. A mining story of great power and interest. The strange characters and experiences one meets with in the mines and among the miners are photographed with absolute fidelity to life. Cloth, 12mo. One Dollar.

AT THE TEMPLE GATES.

By Dr. J. Stewart Doubleday. These are songs partly of the heart and partly of the imagination. The taste of the author is seen in every line, as also is his culture. Cloth, 12mo. One Dollar.

AUNT LUCY'S CABIN.

By Mrs. E. R. Turner. An interesting and dramatic dialogue, worked out with considerable attention to detail. The characters are not numerous, but there are enough of them to make the pages of the little volume sparkle with animation. Cloth, small 12mo. Fifty Cents.

BY THEIR FRUITS.

By Edith M. Nicholl. Is a strong story of a modern type, full of incident and with a heart throb in every page. This novel is sure to make a sensation by virtue of its inherent power. Cloth, 12mo. One Dollar.

CASE OF EXPEDIENCE, A.

By Marie E. Richard. This is a novel which deals with questions of expedience in connection with seminary and church life and duty. The heroine has a call and a mission, and in her choice of a career has to battle with manifold prejudices and misconceptions. Cloth, 12mo. One Dollar.

CITY BOYS' LIFE IN THE COUNTRY;

or, Howard and Weston at Bedford. By Clinton Osgood Burling. Is a book that appeals to every true boy. One can fairly scent the odor of the violets and wood anemones along the banks of the trout streams and hear the noisy chatter of the red squirrels. Bill's story of the Chinese pirates, and his valuable information on hunting, fishing and ornithology hold the interest of the reader from the beginning to the end. Cloth, 12mo. Illustrated. One Dollar.

DOLINDA AND THE TWINS.

By Dora Harvey Munyon. Like Mrs. Munyon's other book, entitled "Half Hour Stories," this volume shows a rare acquaintance with human life and motives, and is written with feminine deftness and insight. Cloth, 12mo. Seventy-five Cents.

ADDENDA.

EGYPTIAN RING, THE.

By Mrs. Nellie Tolman Sawyer. An occult story which opens in the State of Massachusetts and ends in the estate of matrimony, and whirls the reader from Boston to Cairo in a breathless and bewildering way. Cloth, small 12mo. Fifty Cents.

EVERYDAY CHILDREN.

By May C. Emmel. This is a very sweet story, and exhibits the strong and weak points of the average child in the every-day home. It appeals with peculiar strength to the feminine heart, and all mothers, sisters and aunts will specially appreciate it. Cloth, small 12mo. Fifty Cents.

LITTLE CRUSADERS, THE.

By Isabel S. Stone. This book deals with one of the most inter-esting and peculiar episodes of the Middle Ages, viz., the marches and countermarches of the Little Crusaders. The author's style is animated and her spirit is sympathetic and yet historical. The work fills a place in literature. Cloth, 12mo. One Dollar.

MUSICAL REFORMATION, A.

By John A. Cone. The story which gives the title to this volume and the stories which follow it are all drawn from real life, and point a moral and adorn a tale. They must be read to be appre-ciated, as they abound in humor and in sharp hits at current follies. Twenty-five Cents.

REALITY AND OTHER POEMS.

By Duncan F. Young. The author of this volume is known throughout Dixie as the "Southern banker poet," and, as in the banking house, so on the sides of Mount Parnassus, his notes are golden. Cloth, small 12mo. Seventy-five Cents.

THREE FAIR PHILANTHROPISTS.

By Alice M. Muzzy. This is a novel full of kindly satire. It exploits the fads and follies of pseudo philanthropists of the boudoir, and yet it is done so gently that there is no bitterness in the laugh. Cloth, 12mo. $1.50.

UNIQUE TALES.

By Ludwig Nicolovius. These tales are unique in fact as in name. They run from the positive through the comparative to the superlative degree. Each reader will have his preference, but will concede that all are good. Cloth, small 12mo. Fifty Cents.

WHAT WILL SHE DO?

By Margaret D. Simms. This is a Southern story of rare in-terest. The heroine enters the service of a prominent family down in Dixie as a governess, and has various experiences which oblige her to leave that position, and which eventually land her in the position of a wife. Cloth, 12mo. One Dollar.

Check Out More Titles From HardPress Classics Series In this collection we are offering thousands of classic and hard to find books. This series spans a vast array of subjects — so you are bound to find something of interest to enjoy reading and learning about.

Subjects:
Architecture
Art
Biography & Autobiography
Body, Mind &Spirit
Children & Young Adult
Dramas
Education
Fiction
History
Language Arts & Disciplines
Law
Literary Collections
Music
Poetry
Psychology
Science
…and many more.

Visit us at www.hardpress.net

CPSIA information can be obtained
at www.ICGtesting.com
Printed in the USA
BVHW041333280819
556932BV00024B/4331/P

9 780371 007686